VIRGINIA WOOLF

FOR BEGINNERS

**AARON
ROSENBLATT**

**ILLUSTRATED BY
AOMI ROSENBLATT**

Writers and Readers

WRITERS AND READERS PUBLISHING, INCORPORATED
One West 125th Street
Dr. Martin Luther King, Jr. Blvd.
New York, N.Y. 10027

A Writers and Readers Documentary Comic Book
Copyright © 1984

ISBN 0 86316 133 2
2 3 4 5 6 7 8 9 0

Manufactured in the United States of America

ACKNOWLEDGEMENTS

I wish to thank Gillian Barlow, Quentin Bell and Glenn Thompson for their generous help in preparing this book for publication.

Thanks to Sarah Haviland, Alexander Plunkett and Sheila White Samton for visual material and feedback.

Thanks specifically to Judy Rosenblatt for the photographs of Asheham, Dalington and Gordon Square.

Aaron Rosenblatt is Professor at the Rockefeller College of Public Affairs and Policy, S.U.N.Y., Albany. He studied at Columbia University and received his doctorate in 1965. A native of Detroit, he now lives with his wife in Albany. Dr. Rosenblatt is presently on sabbatical, with an appointment as Senior Fellow at the Rockefeller Institute of Government.

Naomi Rosenblatt gingerly agreed to collaborate with her father on this book. She found him surprisingly cooperative. After graduating from The Cooper Union in 1979, she has worked as a freelance visual artist in capacities ranging from corporate muralist to teacher. *Zen for Beginners* was her first illustrated book, this is her second. A native New Yorker, Naomi hopes to remain in Manhattan until it becomes obsolete for her income bracket.

Dedicated, with love and gratitude,
to the memory of
Diana Rosenblatt

TABLE OF CONTENTS

1. INTRODUCTION

Virginia Woolf. Her name brings to mind many different images. Most are positive, some negative.

Here is Virginia Woolf, aged 28, the fun-loving tweaker of official noses, blacking her face, donning a false beard and moustache, cross-dressing in a caftan and turban, masquerading as an Ethiopian prince, a silent member of a seemingly solemn diplomatic mission, ceremoniously piped aboard H.M.S. *Dreadnought*, in cahoots with her brother Adrian and his friend Duncan Grant, creating a hoax that was reported on the front pages of London newspapers. The spoof embarrassed the Admiralty and the officers in charge of the British Home Fleet by demonstrating their vulnerability to the high jinks of undergraduates.

Three years later in 1913, aged 31, soon after becoming a Socialist, she describes herself attending a meeting of the Women's Co-operative Guild, listening to a group of earnest working-class women, their "very names like the stones in the fields," touching nothing lightly, gripping "pencils as if they were brooms," heavy women, vigorous, independent, gifted with a native humor, instructing her on the importance of divorce, education, the vote—"all good things" for women.

Eighteen years later, aged 49, she presents us with another image of herself at another public meeting. This time she is the speaker, an ardent feminist addressing the London Society for Women's Service, urging them to kill the Angel in the House, that creature from the Victorian age who advised women, above all else, to be pleasing to men, to be tender and to flatter, to use their wiles and their arts to disguise the fact that women have a mind of their own.

Do snuff the bugger!

This Virginia Woolf is tough and determined. She tells an audience of young professional women that they must be prepared to strangle the Angel in the House, for if they do not murder her, the Angel will kill their chance of becoming successful. Followers of this Angel become tender writers anxious to flatter and please their readers, writing sentences not worth the paper covered by their scribbling.

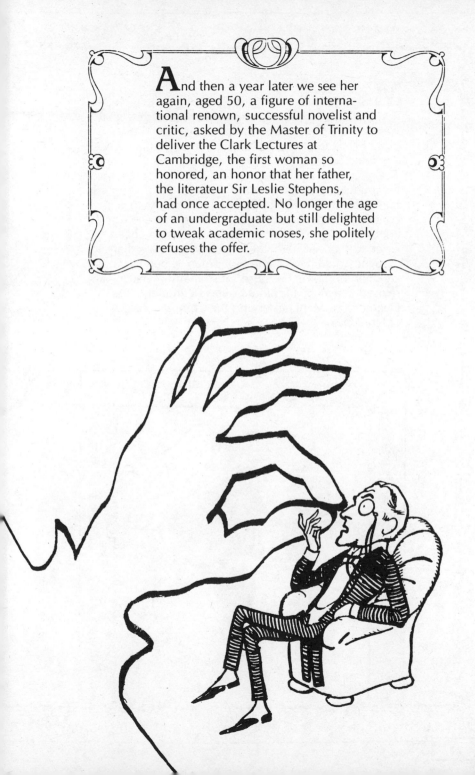

And then a year later we see her again, aged 50, a figure of international renown, successful novelist and critic, asked by the Master of Trinity to deliver the Clark Lectures at Cambridge, the first woman so honored, an honor that her father, the literateur Sir Leslie Stephens, had once accepted. No longer the age of an undergraduate but still delighted to tweak academic noses, she politely refuses the offer.

Most men and women are flattered by the recognition signified by highly sought after honors. Her goal was to avoid the corruption that comes with having a place inside the tent and having to pay the price later when the bill is called. In *A Room of One's Own* and *Three Guineas* she scolds Oxford and Cambridge for the grudging place they set for women. Passing up the honor is a small price to pay for the freedom to continue scolding Oxbridge professors. Yet she was honest enough to note her pleasure at having been asked to succeed her father, the kind of honor that she thought would have made him proud of her. Having kept her thumb on her nose for so many years, she also refused to accept additional offers of an Honorary Degree from Manchester and the Companionship of Honour.

These images of Virginia Woolf have all been positive. We have seen her as an impish spoiler, an ardent feminist and an acclaimed author, uncorrupted by proffered honors and titles. Some of her contemporaries recall her in less heroic guise. To some she is the Invalid Lady of Bloomsbury, the exquisite recluse, excitable, thin-skinned, taking to her bed for days after reading a critical review of one of her novels. To others she is a dull and arty High Priest in the Palace of Art, an ivory-tower aesthete, instructing her betters, giants like Arnold Bennett and H. G. Wells, on ways to improve their novels, presuming to change the form and substance of the English novel, to bleach it of brick and mortar, of business deal and bank account.

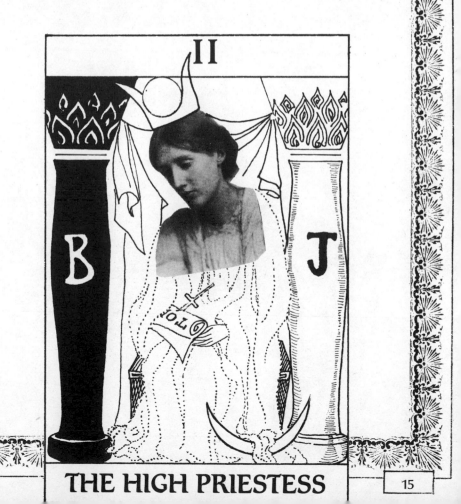

THE HIGH PRIESTESS

Ａnd then there is the nasty picture that she herself created for the amusement of her closest friends— Virginia Woolf, the upper middle-class snob, fawning over shallow women with an aristocratic pedigree, preferring, without any hesitation or misgiving, to attend one of their parties where the Prince of Wales has promised to appear, gleeful at the chance of passing up a meeting with Albert Einstein.

In her diaries and letters, she has left us an album with these many different snapshots. There sits the famous novelist, eyes hooded, stately, her delicate fingers holding a cigarette holder.

Here, sitting beside her depressed father peers the tentative adolescent, cautious, unable to cope with the sudden death of her mother and a beloved stepsister. There is the young bride, frigid, puzzled by the fizzle of sex, consulting her sister Vanessa, asking for advice on ways to make the apparatus begin to work.

She has also left us pictures of the lucid essayist, voyaging through the literature of the past, interviewing Judith, an imaginary sister of Shakespeare, finding out why this talented woman wrote no plays and penned no sonnets.

And then there are the snapshots taken by her husband Leonard in his five-volume autobiography. Now Virginia is a mental patient, Leonard her nurse and psychiatrist, ready to protect her from the hurly-burly of London, and the demands of her friends, always on guard, eager to do battle against her mad impulses, failing, finally, to keep her from packing her pockets with heavy stones and drowning herself in the River Ouse near their country home in Sussex.

All of these images exist side by side because Virginia Woolf was so honest with her readers. Her language blows away smoke screens and any attempt to find a hiding place for herself. Her words are sharp, cutting away the fat and blubber, exposing muscle, sinew, bone. In her autobiographical essays and in her diaries and letters she is the doctor, operating on herself, slicing away at the pomposity of others. Because of her honesty, we have come to know Virginia Woolf better, and to know more about her, than we know about most of our contemporaries, our neighbors hidden behind their curtains, coming outside periodically to make predictions about the weather, our colleagues nattering on about yesterday's television, our relatives treating us to the stale tidbits culled from newspaper columnists.

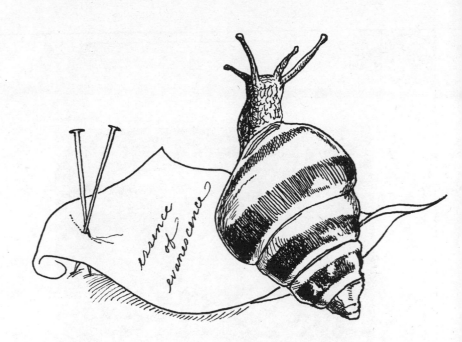

Virginia Woolf, in contrast, never wastes our time. Her thoughts are fresh and hers alone. When she describes a moth beating its wings against a window, or the trail of a snail slowly climbing across a wall, or a mysterious, official car snaking its way through heavy London traffic, she is alive to the potentiality of the moment, struggling to pin down the evanescent, able to discern the timeless in a frivolous pair of grey gloves or a well-prepared family meal.

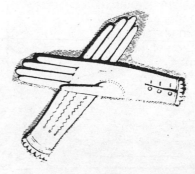

She is a lighthouse, a beacon helping us
to locate ourselves in heavy seas, lighting
up our lives, leading us to an understanding
of the past and an appreciation of the
boundlessness of the present.

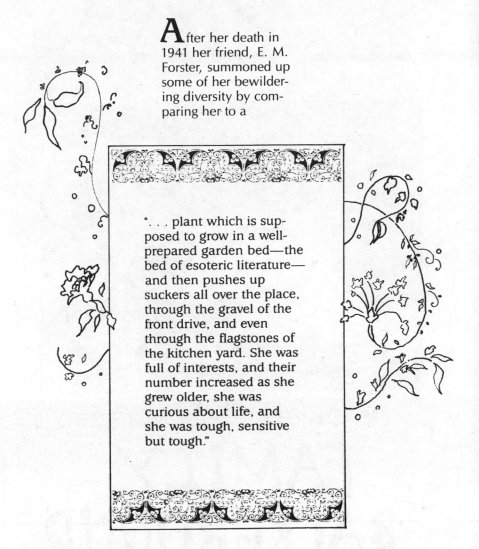

After her death in 1941 her friend, E. M. Forster, summoned up some of her bewildering diversity by comparing her to a

". . . plant which is supposed to grow in a well-prepared garden bed—the bed of esoteric literature—and then pushes up suckers all over the place, through the gravel of the front drive, and even through the flagstones of the kitchen yard. She was full of interests, and their number increased as she grew older, she was curious about life, and she was tough, sensitive but tough."

In this book we try to show these different sides of Virginia Woolf. The final form may not be tidy, but we want the picture to be true to life.

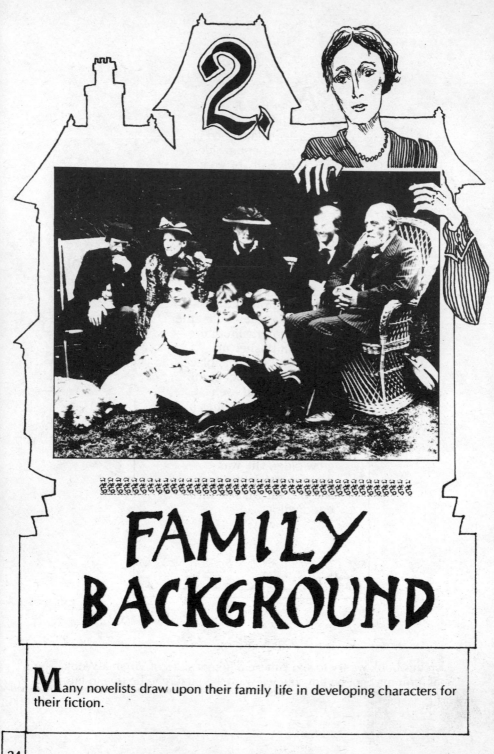

FAMILY BACKGROUND

Many novelists draw upon their family life in developing characters for their fiction.

Perhaps Virginia Woolf's family was more important to her than the families of most writers, since she was educated at home, and much of her life was centered in that large household. Seven maidservants, supported by a squad of older women and lame men who did odd jobs during the day, ministered to the needs of this large, complex family of eleven.

There never seemed to be enough space in the six-story house at 22 Hyde Park Gate. As a teenager fleeing from the unwanted attentions of her stepbrother, Virginia compared herself to an "unfortunate minnow shut up in the same tank with an unwieldy and turbulent whale."

Virginia's parents decided to limit their family after the birth of Vanessa and Thoby. Fortunately, contraceptive practices in the 1880's worked imperfectly, and Adeline Virginia Stephen was born on January 25, 1882, the second daughter and third child of Leslie and Julia Stephen.

Her upper-middle-class family was connected by marriage to the aristocracy; the Duchess of Bedford was first cousin to Virginia's mother. Many of her relatives were high achievers. Her great aunt, Julia Cameron, was a superb photographer. A grandfather and an uncle, a step-brother and her father were all elevated to knighthood, and her aunt Katherine was appointed Principal of Newnham, a college for women at Cambridge.

As a mature woman Virginia sought to account for the success of her male relatives. She believed they had been stamped out and moulded by the patriarchical machinery of their class—gaining favorable reports from schoolmasters, winning scholarship and fellowship awards.

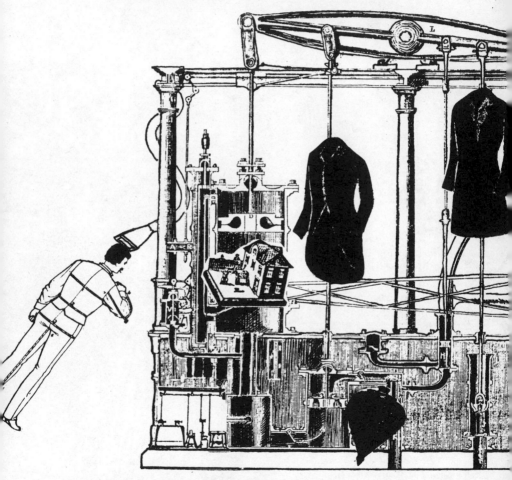

The system worked well for those fortunate enough to be educated at elite schools. At that time the red of the British Empire still appeared on all seven continents of the globe, and the machinery of the Empire created jobs, both at home and overseas, for the sons of England educated at Oxford and Cambridge.

Every one of her relatives, she concluded, was "shot into that machine and came out at the other end, at the age of sixty or so, a Headmaster, an Admiral, a Cabinet Minister, a Judge."

The positions she listed corresponded to appointments actually made to her relatives. For example, one cousin, H.A.L. Fisher, became Warden of New College and President of the Board of Education in the Lloyd George administration; an uncle, James Fitzjames Stephen, was appointed a judge of the High Court.

Her family were members of the intellectual elite of England. They were all well educated, and well read, and the positions they occupied were highly prized. Her father proved himself to be an intellectual by a willingness to take the measure of his contemporaries, not by the conventional standards of birth or wealth, but by their moral achievement and their contribution to society.

Dear Old Ponderous Dad

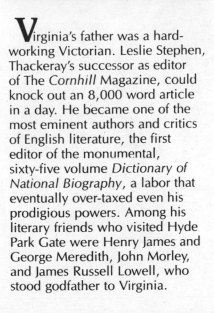

Virginia's father was a hard-working Victorian. Leslie Stephen, Thackeray's successor as editor of The *Cornhill* Magazine, could knock out an 8,000 word article in a day. He became one of the most eminent authors and critics of English literature, the first editor of the monumental, sixty-five volume *Dictionary of National Biography*, a labor that eventually over-taxed even his prodigious powers. Among his literary friends who visited Hyde Park Gate were Henry James and George Meredith, John Morley, and James Russell Lowell, who stood godfather to Virginia.

The Stephen-Duckworth union was a second marriage for both of Virginia's parents. Her mother Julia had been happily married to Herbert Duckworth, handsome, wealthy, a respected barrister. Unexpectedly, in an improbable moment reaching for a fig, he ruptured an abcess and died suddenly, leaving his young wife pregnant, still carrying their third child. Widowed at age twenty-four, her older child three years old, Julia Duckworth was deeply grieved by the death of her husband. Subsequently she told Virginia's father that she had felt so distraught that death would have been the greatest boon that could have been bestowed upon her.

Recalling her intense grief and pleasure she confided to a friend, "I have been as unhappy and as happy as it is possible for a human to be." Her husband's death left her deadened, numbed, desiring death but determined to carry on for the sake of her children, to rear them as best she could rather than shift the burden onto others.

Leslie Stephen's first marriage had been to Thackeray's younger daughter, Harriet Marian, or Minny as she was called. Minny was shy and childlike, with hair the color of bronze and a delicate complexion. It was not immediately evident that their first child Laura was mentally retarded, for her parents took a favorable view of her late development, choosing to look upon her as a "delicate" child. Five years after Laura was born, Minny was again pregnant. She had been ailing, but her death from convulsions was sudden and unexpected. Minny died on her husband's forty-third birthday, a day that Leslie Stephen never again celebrated.

The beautiful young widow Julia—
and the intellectually brilliant Leslie, tall
and lean with a straggling beard, found
themselves neighbors, living in adjacent
houses at Numbers 20 and 22 Hyde Park Gate,
a quiet block near Kensington Gardens.
It was natural for them to be drawn together
and to sympathize with each other's plight.
Their tender feelings grew, and after a
cautious, lengthy courtship, Leslie Stephen
proposed to Julia Duckworth.

At first she refused his offer. His response was to
offer her more time. He was in no hurry, he said, and
suggested that she think of him as he did his old collie,
nice, kind and loving, thankful for whatever affection
he received. Julia finally agreed to marry him. "I will
be your wife and will do my best to be a good wife to
you." They were married on March 26, 1878 and in
less than six years four children were born:
**VANESSA, (1879); THOBY, (1880); VIRGINIA,
(1882); and ADRIAN, (1883).**

The social and intellectual advantages made available by her parents gave Virginia a headstart in life. She was always able to afford a room of her own and to purchase the years needed to learn how to write. There was always enough money to hire servants to cook and clean and care for her needs.

However, her cloistered life at Hyde Park Gate and her position as the youngest daughter in this three-tiered household had their disadvantages. Her step-brothers, George and Gerald, were fourteen and twelve years older than she. Both were attracted by her delicate, flame-colored cheeks, her green eyes, her full lips.

In the last year of her life she recalled a scene from her childhood: her step-brother had lifted her onto a slab used for holding dishes, which was located in the hall outside the dining room. As she sat there Gerald's hand wandered over her body, feeling under her clothes, steadily going up and up, not stopping until his fingers had explored her private parts. She resented the invasion and for years afterward felt ashamed, recognizing at some deep level of her being— acquired, she felt, thousand of years ago—an instinctive dread, a dumb feeling, difficult to express.

At the age of thirteen Virginia suffered another blow from the death of her mother. Julia Stephen had grown exhausted from caring for three families, babying a husband crushed and broken by the self-imposed task of turning out volume after volume for the insatiable *Dictionary*. After her death a dark cloud settled over the family. A finger of silence crossed their lips, a mute injunction to repress their feelings. Suffering in silence, they remained enveloped in a haze of heavy emotions.

Slowly the funeral atmosphere lifted as the family members were drawn into the courtship and marriage of Virginia's stepsister Stella to the dashing Jack Hills.

Their relief was shortlived. In July 1897, three months after her marriage, Stella, now pregnant, was taken ill with appendicitis. Her doctor mismanaged both conditions. Suddenly Stella died, and the family was once again plunged into gloom.

Leslie Stephen now became an old, unhappy man, lonely, deserted, angry and despairing, increasingly deaf, more and more remote from his children. He became unreasonable with Vanessa and then Virginia, overly fearful of being inundated by his daughters' mismanagement of the household accounts.

With his decline her stepbrother George took on the roles of mother and father, introducing eighteen-year-old Virginia to high society, supervising her dress, lavishing her with gifts of jewelry, escorting her to fashionable balls, chiding her to make the most of these opportunities. Virginia was ill at ease in this atmosphere, either tongue-tied at Lady Sligo's or talking too much, to Lady Carnarvon, making what were considered shocking, inappropriate references to Plato.

Years later Virginia wrote of a long unsatisfactory evening spent with George and Lady Carnarvon. Once it was over she looked forward to her bed. She undid the buttons on her white satin dress, unpinned the flowers held in place by her jewelry and slipped off her petticoats. After hanging her white silk stockings over a chair and climbing into bed, she was ready for sleep, anxious to forget her awkwardness at the ball. While drifting off, she was frightened when the door opened. It was George. "Don't turn on the light," he ordered. Murmuring terms of endearment he threw himself on her bed and took her in his arms.

She received further buffeting at age twenty-two upon the death of her father, and two years later upon the sudden death of her older brother Thoby, one of her special heroes. Orphaned, molested, deprived of Stella and Thoby, Virginia was never again to feel fully safe in an insecure world. As these losses piled up, she became vulnerable, unable to handle the stress of life, from time to time losing control and succumbing to mental illness.

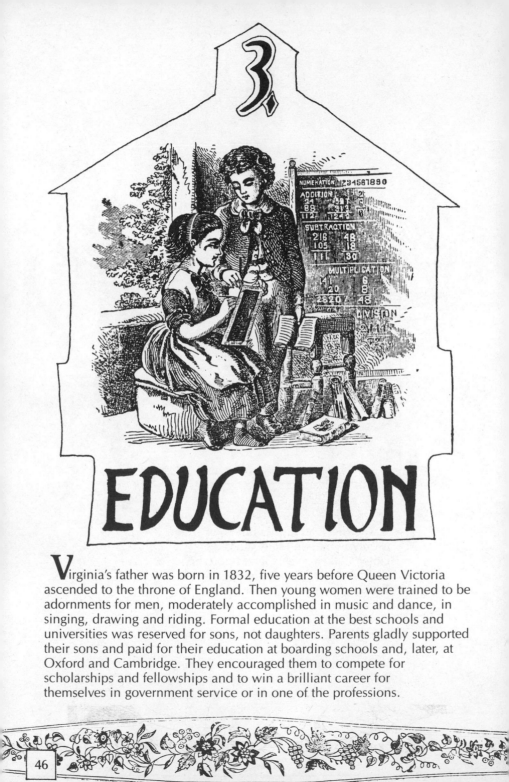

EDUCATION

Virginia's father was born in 1832, five years before Queen Victoria ascended to the throne of England. Then young women were trained to be adornments for men, moderately accomplished in music and dance, in singing, drawing and riding. Formal education at the best schools and universities was reserved for sons, not daughters. Parents gladly supported their sons and paid for their education at boarding schools and, later, at Oxford and Cambridge. They encouraged them to compete for scholarships and fellowships and to win a brilliant career for themselves in government service or in one of the professions.

To Virginia's mother the highest expression of a women's nature was the rendering of service to others, her husband and children and those who found themselves in less fortunate circumstances. In *To The Lighthouse*, a fictional but essentially autobiographical account of summers spent at St. Ives, Cornwall, Virginia draws a portrait of her mother in the guise of Mrs. Ramsay. Her day is stitched together by a succession of good works and good deeds—soothing the ruffled feathers of a priggish young academician; helping one son dissolve his anger toward his father; practicing the art of matchmaking by bringing a young couple together; knitting a sock for the little boy at the lighthouse threatened with a tubercular hip; always reassuring her husband that his work was first-class, that his contribution was highly respected by his peers.

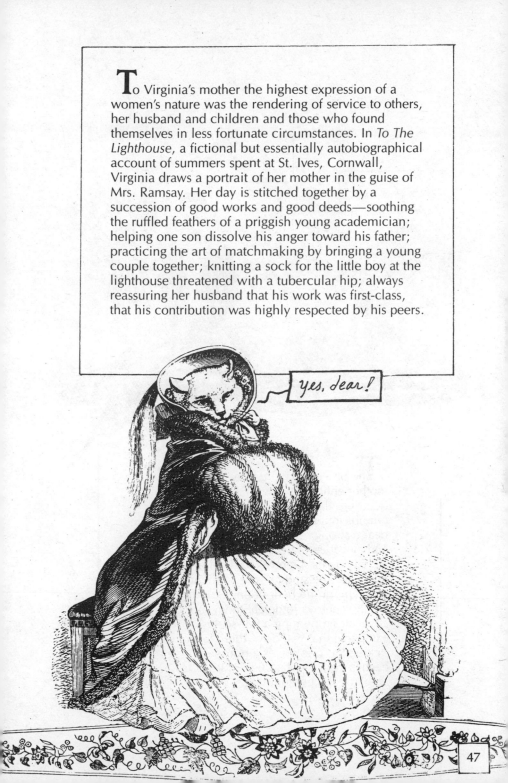

yes, dear!

The one book written by Virginia's mother entitled *Notes for Sick Rooms* describes the miseries wrought by bed crumbs in a style that years later will bear a strong resemblance to the wit and elegance of her daughter. Julia Stephen twits scientists for having neglected the study of this tormenting problem for the bedridden. Crumbs are the enemy! To defeat them she advocates mounting a full-scale campaign that will drive them from the sick bed as one drives a horde of beetles from a potato field. Her notes are light and entertaining.

Nonetheless, Julia Stephen was entirely serious about wanting her daughters to dedicate themselves to a life of service. She deeply believed that in serving others women fulfill their highest nature.

Writing was the profession to which Virginia dedicated herself. Speaking in 1931 before a group of women with professional careers about her experience as a writer and book reviewer, she recalled the special problems caused by the Angel that once resided in every respectable Victorian house. This Angel was the ideal of womanhood encouraged by a number of British social institutions: the Empire and its Colonies, Queen Victoria and Alfred Lord Tennyson, with additional strength drawn from the growing middle classes.

Christina Rossetti expressed
the Angel's attitude
about the relationships
between men and women:

Woman was made for man's delight
Charm O woman be not afraid;
His shadow by day, his moon by night
Woman was made.

When Virginia began writing reviews of books written by men, for journals and newspapers edited by men, the Angel advised her, above all else, to be pleasing to men: "Be sympathetic; be tender; flatter." Virginia was told to pretend not to have any ideas of her own. Lastly, the Angel advised, "Be pure."

Possessing an independent income, Virginia felt herself free of the need to heed the Angel, to tell lies to her readers. She did more than discard the Angel's advice. Virginia Woolf told her audience that she turned upon the Angel, caught her by the throat and strangled her on the spot. Were she ever to be charged in a court of law with murder of this hypothetical monster, she would build her case around having acted in self-defense.

Portrait of the Angel as Death the Reaper

Otherwise, the Angel would have killed Virginia Woolf, the writer, as she had murdered countless women writers, painters and musicians. Autobiographical accounts of women artists who were Virginia's contemporaries report on the many obstacles they were forced to overcome in order to make a career for themselves.

*Here Rests
Judith Shakespeare*

Virginia resented the generally-accepted rule that barred women in Victorian England from enrolling at the traditional colleges comprising Oxford and Cambridge. In *A Room of One's Own* she creates a satirical drama set on the lawn at "Oxbridge" where she is thinking about a talk to be delivered at "Fernham," a school like Newnham and Girton, two colleges at Cambridge which admitted women.

HALT!!!

Lost in thought, she wanders, across a grassy plot when an officer of the University, a Beadle, takes after her. "I was a woman. This was the turf; there was the path. Only the Fellows and Scholars are allowed here; the gravel is the place for me."

Where's your escort, Duckie?

Another rebuff awaits her at the door of the library. A kindly old gentleman standing guard there is under orders to refuse her entry. Women are admitted to the library only when accompanied by a Fellow of the College.

The meals prepared for women attending Fernham are also demeaning. Dinner begins with a plain gravy soup served in a plain dish. The main course of beef, greens and potatoes lacks inspiration as do the prunes and custard for dessert. Instead of a carafe of wine, a jug of water circulates among the diners. Virginia sums up the effect of such meals on young women students: "One cannot think well, love well, sleep well, if one has not dined well." Meanwhile, at the Oxbridge Commons young men are dining on a succulent salmon, or a sole covered with the whitest cream sauce, on a fat, crisp partridge and potato slices, thin as coins, but soft and buttery.

Virginia's education as the daughter of Leslie Stephen was much less deprived than the one Fernham students received in *A Room of One's Own*. Having heard from her older brother Thoby, home from boarding school, about the pleasures of reading Homer, Virginia, already receiving instruction in Latin, asked for and received private tutoring in Greek. Moreover, her father respected her intellect and her interest in literature. On her ninth birthday he remarked proudly to his wife, "She is very much like me." At age fifteen she was free to read any book selected from his extensive library.

Beside granting her this freedom, her father also chose certain books for her which reflected confidence in her intelligence: Froude's *Carlyle*, Creighton's *Queen Elizabeth*, James Russell Lowell's *Poems*, Macauley's *History*; Carlyle's *French Revolution*, Arnold's *History of Rome*, his own biography of his friend, Henry Fawcett and many others. The agreement reached was that she would discuss these books with him.

His single advice on reading was sound. "But, my dear, if it's worth reading, it's worth reading twice." He encouraged her to express her opinion about the merits of each book. As they discussed fictional characters and actions, as well as incidents drawn from their everyday life, she learned to distinguish between selfish, trivial opinions and those informed by ethical values.

"But my dear, if it's worth reading, it's worth reading twice."

For example, an acquaintance of her father complained about the wet weather that had been casting a cloud over her tour of Cornwall. Leslie Stephen never fancied himself a democrat. Yet all of his sympathies lay not with the traveler out-of-sorts, but with the poor farmer whose crop might be spoiled by the heavy rains. He then proceeded to express his views to the woman even though he knew she would find them unpleasant.

Isn't it wretched?!

Leslie Stephen was also willing to risk a hostile reception to his writing, to challenge conventional values and reevaluate authors with well-established reputations—qualities later evident in Virginia Woolf's essays and reviews.

As part of her education he advised Virginia to read what she liked, for no better reason than she liked it. She was never to pretend to admire work that did not please her. These were his simple lessons in the art of reading.

Lessons in the art of writing were equally brief.

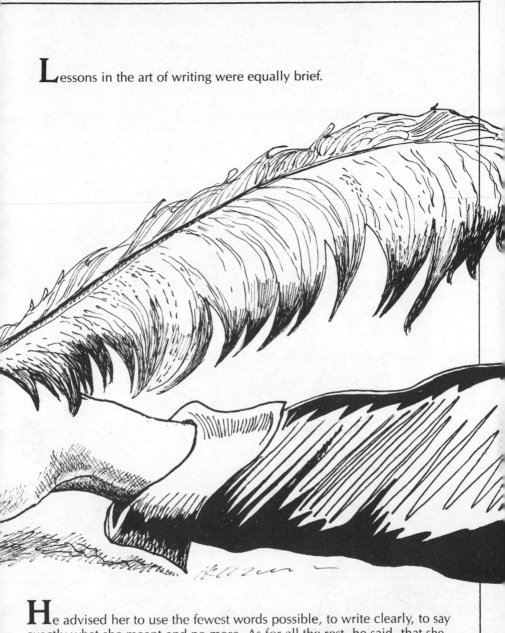

He advised her to use the fewest words possible, to write clearly, to say exactly what she meant and no more. As for all the rest, he said, that she must learn for herself. As a critic he passed along one sound piece of advice to authors, which he himself tried to follow in his own life: authors should dare to be themselves.

By not attending a famous university
Virginia was deprived of an opportunity to
compete with her contemporaries, to
toughen herself for the struggle all writers
face. Nonetheless, the encouragement,
attention and respect received at home
and the education gained from studying
literature with the most distinguished
man of letters in England proved to be
a fair trade. Neither she nor her father ever
put much stock in the benefit of university
lectures for students.

*They're a pack
of horses' arses!!*

After having delivered the first
series of Clark lectures, he
concluded that his audience
could have learned all he had to
say by reading two or three
books, which would have taken
half the time spent in attending
the lectures.

Once she became a successful author, Virginia Woolf expressed doubt that most teachers—middlebrows—could teach anyone how to read critically. The way to learn to read Shakespeare, she counseled, was to buy a good, cheap edition of his plays and then sit down and read them. If readers had trouble understanding Hamlet, they should get to know him, invite him to tea, spend some time with him. She also had doubts that anyone could teach someone else how to write. Her father's lessons had been short and simple and helpful. The rest was best left to the would-be writer.

Virginia missed meeting students her own age and testing out her ideas through challenge and argument. Once she began meeting her brothers' and sister's friends, first at 22 Hyde Park Gate in Kensington and then at their new home at 46 Garden Square in Bloomsbury, she was able to make up for this deficit in her education.

4. MENTAL ILLNESS

Everyone who grows to maturity must pass through a number of difficult times and learn to cope with loss, lovers who have strayed or parents, brothers and sisters who have died before their time. Sometimes pain comes from the lash of criticism, harsh words from a father, biting deep, making a child doubtful, shaken by a sudden flood of depression and worthlessness. Every child can recall special episodes of pain.

Virginia was more vulnerable than most children to the inevitable tragedies of family life. Her mother died when she was thirteen years old. "Her death," she said, "was the greatest disaster that could happen." Many children lose a mother or father, and a few lose both parents, without suffering a nervous breakdown as Virginia did.

Not all children are plunged into a period of deep mourning as intense as the one her father draped over the Stephen household. Becoming more and more deaf, the groans of Leslie Stephen were louder than he realized. Twice a widower, her father felt guilty at having failed to show his second wife enough affection during her lifetime, of having failed to tell her how much he loved her.

Wanting perhaps to demonstrate her sympathy, Virginia exhibited symptoms showing she was more troubled than her father. Now she herself became the most disturbed member of the family, displaying a series of nervous signs to others. Virginia was deeply depressed; Virginia was terrified of other people. When spoken to, she blushed scarlet. Her pulse raced. Worst of all, she experienced a feeling of terror listening to those horrid internal voices telling her things no one else could hear. The family doctor put a stop to all her lessons, the first of many restrictions in her daily life. All of the doctors who subsequently treated her favored this kind of prescription.

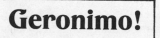

Geronimo!

A second more serious breakdown occurred in 1904 soon after the death of her father. She loved him more than her sister Vanessa or her brother Adrian did and was exhausted, overly strained by his lingering on before dying of cancer. Once again she heard insistent voices urging her to commit foolish acts. The voices were punishing her for past indulgences. In order to pacify them, she made an effort to stop eating. For the first time in her life she tried to commit suicide.

μετεδίδοσαν ἀλλήλοις ὧν εἶχον

ξύλα δ' ἦν ἐν τῷ σταθμῷ πολλά· οἱ δὲ ὀψὲ προσιόι
ξύλα οὐκ εἶχον. Οἱ οὖν πάλαι ἥκοντες καὶ τὸ

The attempted suicide may have been more a gesture than a serious effort; the window from which she jumped was low enough to the ground so that the fall did not cause her any serious harm. Lying in bed, distraught, she thought the birds outside her room were singing to one another in Greek, while King Edward VII, hiding among the azalea bushes, was talking dirty.

Virginia broke down a third time in 1910. The immediate occasion for this episode seemed to stem from her fears about the anticipated reaction of readers critical of her first novel, *The Voyage Out*, which she expected to finish soon. Also, she was feeling guilty over a flirtation she and her brother-in-law Clive Bell were carrying on while his wife was engrossed in mothering her first born. Later Virginia admitted that her own thoughtlessness and disloyalty at that time "turned more of a knife in me than anything else has ever done." Vanessa was hurt and disappointed by Virginia's behavior and upon Dr. Savage's advice arranged for her to enter a private nursing home, Burley Park at Twickenham.

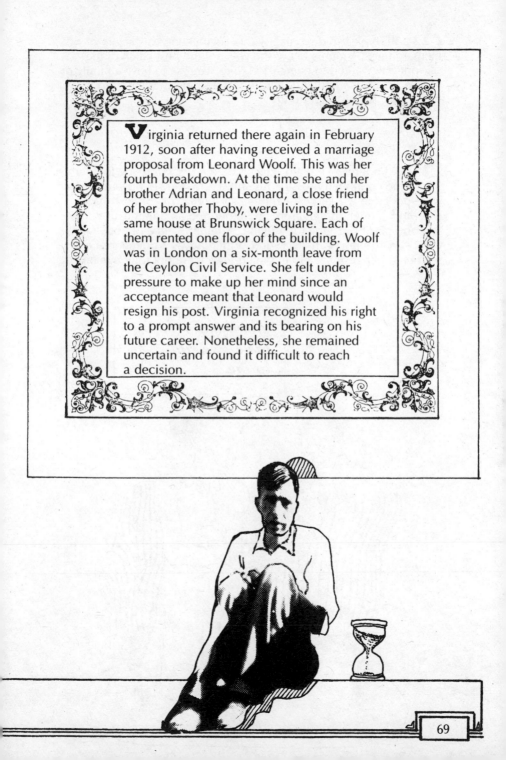

Virginia returned there again in February 1912, soon after having received a marriage proposal from Leonard Woolf. This was her fourth breakdown. At the time she and her brother Adrian and Leonard, a close friend of her brother Thoby, were living in the same house at Brunswick Square. Each of them rented one floor of the building. Woolf was in London on a six-month leave from the Ceylon Civil Service. She felt under pressure to make up her mind since an acceptance meant that Leonard would resign his post. Virginia recognized his right to a prompt answer and its bearing on his future career. Nonetheless, she remained uncertain and found it difficult to reach a decision.

As a thirty-year-old woman with a seventeen-year history of mental illness, Virginia knew she was not the best catch of the season. She wanted to be married, like Vanessa to have a family of her own, to be settled and secure. What, then, made her hesitate? Why not grab this opportunity?

She did not love Leonard. His kisses left her cold. She told him so, but he continued pressing his suit. Furthermore, his prospects were poor. He was almost penniless. Virginia, in contrast, had inherited enough money from her father and an aunt never to have to worry about working for a living. Another source of uncertainty was Leonard's Jewish background. Virginia was a member of a segment of English society in which Jews were not fully integrated.

After overcoming her doubts, Virginia
Stephen and Leonard Woolf were married at
the Register Office in the District of St.
Pancras in the County of London on August
10, 1912. With her marriage Virginia
acquired not only a husband but also a
nurse-caretaker, an overseer-chamberlain
who felt himself fully capable of regulating
her existence for the rest of her life.

It was Leonard who decided how late she could stay at parties, and when it was time for her to leave. And after her fifth breakdown it would be Leonard who decided that they should move from Bloomsbury to Richmond, far enough from family and friends, to make it unlikely for them to drop in unexpectedly and disrupt the routine he had established for her. Perhaps of greatest importance, it was Leonard who decided she was not well enough to have children or raise a family.

Living under this careful regimen eventually worked out to Virginia's advantage. But first she had to become accustomed to the change and to accept the new arrangements that Leonard was prescribing. This took time and was achieved only after great personal struggle.

On September 9, 1913 after only thirteen months of marriage, Virginia felt defeated and tried to commit suicide. This attempt was much more serious than the first. This time she swallowed a hundred grams of veronal, a dose large enough to kill her.

Fortunately, Geoffrey Keynes, a friend living at Brunswick Square, was a house surgeon at St. Bartolomew's. He and Leonard rushed to the hospital and obtained a pump which the doctors and nurses used to empty the drug from her stomach. It took several hours before they were able to save her life.

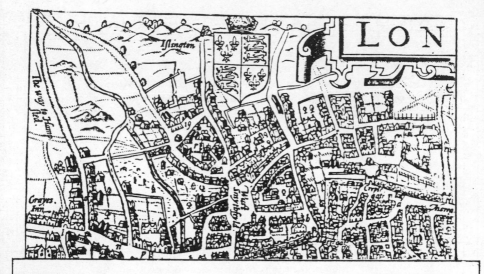

During this fifth mental breakdown Virginia Woolf was so disturbed that she could not return to the nursing home at Twickenham. As her husband, Leonard then had to decide whether or not he should ask to have her certified and to request admission to an insane asylum. He was relieved of the need to make this decision when Virginia's stepbrother George offered them the use of his large house in Sussex.

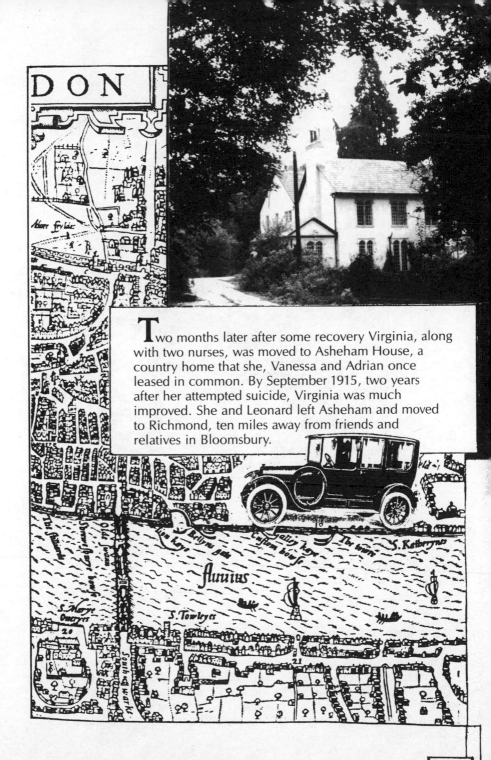

Two months later after some recovery Virginia, along with two nurses, was moved to Asheham House, a country home that she, Vanessa and Adrian once leased in common. By September 1915, two years after her attempted suicide, Virginia was much improved. She and Leonard left Asheham and moved to Richmond, ten miles away from friends and relatives in Bloomsbury.

Throughout the rest of her life Virginia remained subject to periodic bouts of mental disturbance. After 1915, however, these episodes were not comparable either in severity or duration to the one suffered during her fifth breakdown.

For the next twenty-five years while under Leonard's care she was able to carry on with her work as a writer, usually with only brief interruptions. Whenever she was upset, Leonard insisted that she stop writing. For most of that time, however, she was well enough to work, as is shown by this computation: From 1915–1939 she was ill on average almost two days a month. This record compares favorably with that of working women in Great Britain who during the 1970's were ill on average one and a half days a month.

In writing her novels Virginia drew upon her memories of mental anguish and her experience with the psychiatrists who treated her. Rachel, the heroine in *The Voyage Out*, sick with a high fever, hallucinates in ways familiar to Virginia. In *Mrs. Dalloway*, Septimus Smith, a young veteran overwhelmed by memories of killing and mutilation witnessed during World War I, hears voices and, like Virginia soon after her mother's death, grows numb, losing the power to taste and to feel.

Her disparaging portraits of two doctors responsible for treating Septimus, Dr. Holmes and the specialist Sir William Bradshaw, show her low assessment of the psychiatric profession. Instead of focusing his attention on the sick patient, Dr. Holmes lets his mind wander over some objects in a fine old Bloomsbury house, tapping a wall to locate the fine panelling hidden beneath the wallpaper instead of examining his patient with equal care to determine the malady underlying his symptoms.

Besides attacking the arrogance of psychiatry in her characterization of Sir William Bradshaw, Virginia Woolf also exposes the services psychiatrists perform as minions of society, helping to preserve and maintain the social order:

Worshipping proportion, Sir William not only prospered himself but made England prosper, secluded her lunatics, forbade childbirth, penalized despair, made it impossible for the unfit to propagate their views until they, too, shared his sense of proportion . . . not only did his colleagues respect him, his subordinates fear him, but the friends and relations of his patients felt for him the keenest gratitude for insisting that these prophetic Christs and Christesses, who prophesied the end of the world, or the advent of God, should drink milk in bed, as Sir William ordered. Sir William with his thirty years' experience of these kinds of cases, and his infallible instinct, this is madness, this sense, his sense of proportion.

Whatever happened to Virginia, no matter how painful or personal, she subjected the experience to inspection and analysis before objectifying it. When the time came she drew upon these experiences for the enrichment of her fiction and her reminiscences.

5. MARRIAGE

It will be interesting!

On May 29, 1912 Virginia Stephen told Leonard Woolf that she would marry him.

Her nephew Quentin Bell, whom Leonard selected to write her authorized biography, considered it "the wisest decision of her life." It was an odd marriage, like most of those among their circle of friends. Marital fidelity, jingoistic patriotism and religious piety found little favor in Bloomsbury. For example, Freud's English translator, James Strachey, visiting his brother Lytton at his country home, once left a room in protest while a guest was testifying to his belief in God. Afterwards, partially in jest, Strachey excused his rudeness saying, "I make it a point never to stay in the room with a Christian."

Leonard Woolf expressed his animus against religion more formally. On the second page of his autobiography he posts this warning about his beliefs:

"The adulation of the deity as creator of the universe in Jewish and Christian psalms and hymns, and indeed by most religions, seems to me ridiculous . . . If there is a purpose in the universe and a creator, both are unintelligible to us."

The correlation between belief in God and marital infidelity is considerably less than perfect. Virginia's father, an acknowledged atheist, was faithful to his wife. His lack of faith never undermined his opinion about proper conduct between ladies and gentlemen. Nonetheless, extramarital affairs often acquire a quasi-legitimacy when the sacrament of marriage and the sanctity of this special relationship are deprived of religious support.

The marriage of Virginia's sister Vanessa to Clive Bell and of Vita Sackville-West to Harold Nicolson demonstrate the wide variations from the Victorian norm of marriage which were common among Virginia's relatives and close friends.

Vanessa and Clive Bell had been married for only thirteen months when Virginia's brother-in-law began to chase after her. Because of Virginia's squeamishness the planned seduction remained at the level of flirtation without blossoming into a full affair. After this, Vanessa's marriage lost its monogamous character. Having lived together as man and wife for five years Clive and Vanessa reached an amicable agreement to continue their marriage in name only. Clive proceeded to indulge in a succession of love affairs over the next three decades. Vanessa, in contrast, practiced a limited form of serial monogamy. For a few years she allowed the distinguished art critic Roger Fry to become her lover. He was dismissed in favor of the artist Duncan Grant, with whom she shared her home until her death.

Clive was the father of Julian and Quentin Bell, and Duncan, the true father of Angelica, Vanessa's third child. Within the Bell family the pretense generally agreed upon was to pass Clive off as the biological father. Unaware of the deception, Angelica felt a special affinity for Duncan at an early age, but grew up believing Clive was her father. Bisexual, with strong homosexual desires, Duncan was not physically attracted to Vanessa. After confessing his inability to remain faithful, Duncan agreed to continue living with Vanessa, and she allowed him to bring his lovers into their home. David Garnett, one of Duncan's young lovers, later married his daughter Angelica. Years earlier Vanessa had turned down Garnett's offer to sleep with her.

Vita Sackville-West was a poet and novelist; her husband Harold Nicolson, a diplomat and statesman. Although their marriage produced two children, both were physically attracted to members of their own sex. In time Vita came to feel that the physical act of heterosexual love as bestial. In her novel *Grand Canyon* one of the characters expresses a similar sentiment,

"One wonders how they ever brought themselves to commit the grotesque act necessary to beget children."

Fortunately, her husband was not a passionate lover. According to their son Nigel, the author of a biography of their marriage, "sex was as incidental," to his father, "and about as pleasurable, as a quick visit to a picture gallery between trains."

Marriage and sex constituted separate domains for this couple. Nicolson referred to Vita's sexual affairs as her "muddles." She referred to his as "fun." These terms reflect their casual, carefree attitude. Sometimes on the same weekend the separate lovers of Harold and Vita would make up a foursome at their home without any jealousy or embarrassment evident among them.

Nigel Nicolson believed that the Woolf and Nicolson "marriages were alike in the freedom they allowed each other, in the invincibility of their love, in its intellectual, spiritual and nonphysical base, in the eagerness of all four of them to savour life, challenge convention, work hard, play dangerously with the emotions—and in their solicitude for each other . . . There was no jealousy between the Woolfs and Nicolsons because they had arrived independently at the same definition of 'trust'."

The Nicolson correspondence contains a much fuller account of their marriage and the love affair between Virginia and Vita than does the record left by the Woolfs. Leonard was eighty years old when he began publishing his autobiography. One can find excuses in 1960 for an old man's decision to exclude detailed discussions of his wife's love affair with a woman. As a young man Leonard was also circumspect about certain items entered into his diary. He took the further precaution of guarding access to entries about Virginia's illness by writing in a code made up of letters from the Tamil and Sinhalese alphabets, languages in which he gained fluency during his stay in Ceylon.

At times Virginia made malicious comments in her diary about family members and friends. Comments about Leonard, however, seldom show evidence of her acid tongue. Like Isa Oliver, the unhappy wife in *Between the Acts* who hid her poetry from her husband, Virginia usually kept such criticisms hidden. Most diary entries about her marriage testify to her happiness. In 1929 she is "the happiest woman . . . The happiest wife, the happiest writer, the most liked inhabitant in Tavistock Square." Fifteen months later she rings up another sale for her happy marriage: "I dare-say few women are happier . . . I have had a good draught of human life, and find much champagne in it. It has not been dull— my marriage; not at all."

Amount-Purchased

Happy Marriage

Despite such reassuring entries other sources, including the unhappy marriages repeatedly depicted in her novels, yield testimony that her marriage was incomplete.

Virginia was sexually frigid. "Why do you think people make such a fuss about marriage and copulation?" she asks innocently in a letter to a friend written while on her honeymoon. Early in the marriage she and Leonard stopped sleeping together. No lusty marriages are depicted in her novels. Most of her characters are lonely. In *Between the Acts*, her last novel, Isa's husband Giles says, "I'm damnable unhappy." Isa agrees. "They were all caught and caged," notes the author.

"Why do you think people make such a fuss about marriage and copulation?"

In the same novel Virginia draws attention
to the sharp differences between Bartolomew
Oliver and his sister Lucy (Leonard and Virginia lived
like brother and sister during most of their marriage).
"What she saw, he didn't; what he saw, she didn't—
and so on *ad infinitum*."

irginia portrays similar differences
between a newly married couple in
the short story, "Lappin and Lapinova."
The character Edward Thorburn bears
a clear resemblance to Leonard Woolf.
Like Leonard he has blue eyes and a
very firm mouth. Edward is thin and
hard and serious. His twitch is
reminiscent of Leonard's inherited
tremor. The author tells her readers
that the newly married couple "were
opposite of each other; he was bold
and determined; she was wary and
undependable. He ruled over the busy
world . . . her world was a desolate,
mysterious place, which she ranged
mostly by moon-light."

Is He A Turn-On?

Leonard Woolf was obstinate and unyielding, acerbic and dour. Only one photograph shows him smiling. His loyalty and uxorious care for Virginia were accompanied with a schoolmaster's passion for control. The regulation exercised over her visits and the curb placed on her playfulness recall the imperial power he exercised over the natives of Hambantota during his tour of duty in Ceylon. Always orderly and organized, he noted in his diary the names of visitors to their home, the number of words he wrote each day, the length of Virginia's menstrual cycle and the fluctuation in her weight.

In small matters he was exacting and tightfisted, demanding that employees account for every half penny, holding himself to the same standard of accountability. During his early years Leonard and Virginia were full owners of the Hogarth Press, which published all of her fiction. Leonard's niece Angelica once asked him for a copy of *Flush* to give to a friend. Instead of granting her request, he sent her home telling her to bring back money to pay for the book. Angelica did as she was told, intimidated by the force of her uncle's personality.

Yes Sir!!!

Aunt Virginia grew more generous as earnings from her novels increased, giving her niece an allowance of £15 every three months. On visits to Vanessa, Virginia sometimes forgot to bring along a check for Angelica. Whenever she asked Leonard to help by making out a check, Angelica noted how long it took him to locate his checkbook and unscrew his fountain pen.

Leonard Woolf was a splendid
nurse-chamberlain, loyal,
dependable, honest and
trustworthy. He helped Virginia
cope with her illness as best he
could. He watched over her
with devotion. Virginia needed
him, but she felt no lust for him.

As an adolescent Virginia had developed crushes on several older women. In her forties she was attracted to the aristocratic Vita Sackville-West, a fullbreasted woman with shapely legs slim as beech trees. To Virginia, Vita was everything she was not; servants and chow dogs heeded her commands; she was the mother of two sons.

Virginia inspired feelings of tenderness in Vita because of her vulnerability. Like Leonard, Vita felt the need to protect Virginia as she spoke of her terror of going mad again. Vita told her husband,

"I'm scared to death of arousing physical feelings in her because of the madness. I don't know what effect it would have . . . it is a fire with which I have no wish to play."

How frigid was Virginia??

O*rlando* was a gift Virginia gave to Vita. Nigel Nicolson termed it "the longest and most charming love letter in literature." This fanciful biography, standing free from limitations of time and gender, begins by chronicling Orlando's (Vita's) life as a young man in the Elizabethan age. At the age of thirty Orlando rises from a deep sleep and finds himself magically transformed into a woman. Vita's mother was not happy that the photographs of Orlando reproduced in the book, are, in fact, photographs of Vita.

Eventually Virginia's love for Vita cooled. While their relationship lasted, Vita was her most exciting love as a mature woman.

BLOOMSBURY FRIENDS

Warmth and attention from family and friends were important necessities for Virginia Woolf. Again and again in her novels she was drawn to write about significant figures in her life—her parents, lovers, friends.

In her Diary she reports thinking of her mother every day until laying this specter permanently to rest after completing *To the Lighthouse*, her fifth novel containing detailed portraits of her mother and father as Mr. and Mrs. Ramsay.

Ralph Denham and his mother, characters in *Night and Day*, her second novel, are based on her husband Leonard and her mother-in-law. In the same novel Katherine Hilbery and her mother bear a strong resemblance to Virginia's aunt, Lady Ritchie. Her brother Thoby, dead before thirty, serves as model for Jacob Flanders in *Jacob's Room*, her third novel, and for Percival in *The Waves*.

One of Virginia's deepest regrets was Leonard's decision not to have children. At 22 Hyde Park Gate she had grown up with seven brothers and sisters in the Duckworth-Stephen household. In the Woolf household at Lexham Gardens Leonard had nine brothers and sisters, and there might have been more if his father had not died suddenly at the age of forty-seven. Their close friend Lytton Strachey grew up at Lancaster Gate in a household of twelve brothers and sisters. These three families contained thirty-one children.

Mid-Victorian families tended to be large. In sharp contrast were the small families produced by the Stephen children and their Bloomsbury friends. Three close friends never married— Lytton Strachey, E. M. Forster and Saxon Sydney-Turner. Marrying late, in his forties, Maynard Keynes and Lydia Lopokova never had issue from their marriage. Although never married, Duncan Grant was the natural father of Angelica Bell. Vanessa's two other children were Julian and Quentin; her brother Adrian's two daughters were Ann and Judith.

Perhaps the continued existence of the Bloomsbury Group resulted, in part from a need of members to create a large extended family none of them proved capable of producing. They replaced ties of blood with ties of friendship, common values and acceptance of a particular style of life. They were bound together by the value of G. E. Moore, the Cambridge philosopher who advocated reliance on reason, not faith, in analyzing moral issues. The most valued states of mind according to Moore were those reserved for contemplating truth, beauty, love.

Not tonight, Deary. I have a headache from contemplating truth, beauty and love!

Bloomsbury never was a
formal group. There were no
admission or discharge ceremonies;
no dues or by-laws; no secret
rings or sacred rituals; no officers
or periodic elections. Historians
use "Bloomsbury" as a shorthand
way of designating an informal,
intimate group of intellectuals,
many of whom were born in
England between 1876–85.

Enjoying gossip, highly critical of one another's work, they were, nonetheless, devoted friends and could be counted on to help each other get through patches of bad times. They remained close for over four decades, much of the time living in London, sometimes in the same block of row houses on Gordon Square, the majority residing in other Bloomsbury squares: Fitzroy, Brunswick, Tavistock.

During summers and on weekends in the country many of them clustered around the South Down of Sussex. The centers there were at Asheham, and later, at Charleston, and Monks House, the homes of Clive and Vanessa Bell and Leonard and Virginia Woolf.

Historians disagree about the exact composition of the Bloomsbury Group since the only membership card was a regular invitation to dinner parties and weekends at these homes. Was E. M. Forster really "in"? Were Charles and Dora Sanger definitely "out"? There is no final answer to such questions. Bloomsbury was part fact and part fiction. Maynard Keynes and Lytton Strachey, Vanessa and Clive, Virginia and Leonard, all wrote personal memoirs about Bloomsbury, tracing its origins, defining its membership, each creating a distinct but overlapping portrait based on memory, experience, desire.

Yet virtually every historian of this period along with the core members of Bloomsbury, the Bloomsberries as Mary MacCarthy dubbed them, (the Bloomsbuggers to envious outsiders) would place the following list of twelve within the inmost circle:

**(1–2) Vanessa and Clive Bell;
(3–4) Virginia and Leonard Woolf;
(5–6) Molly and Desmond MacCarthy;
(7) Virginia's brother Adrian
Stephen, but not his wife
Karin; (8) Maynard Keynes,
but not his wife Lydia;
(9) Roger Fry, but not his
wife or lover, both named
Helen; (10) Lytton Strachey;
(11) Duncan Grant;
(12) Saxon Sydney-Turner.**

(3–4) Virginia and Leonard Woolf

(1–2) Vanessa and Clive Bell

(5–6) Molly and Desmond MacCarthy
(Mary)

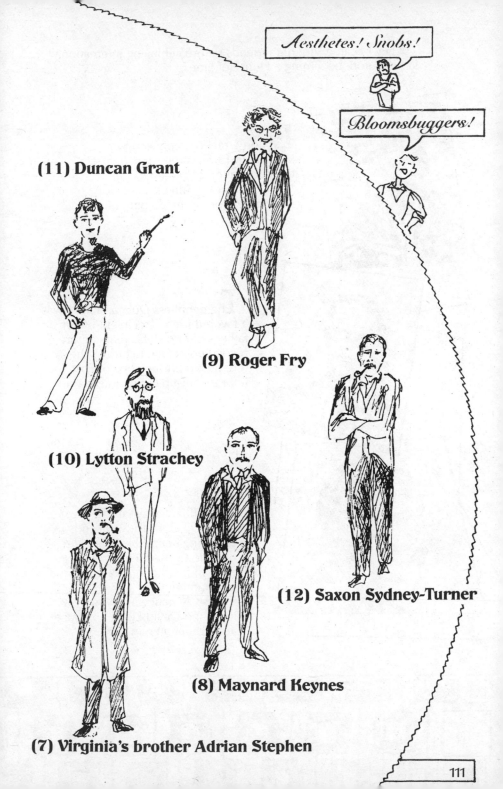

They became Virginia's friends before achieving international fame, before becoming a House of Lions.

Lytton Strachey proposed to Virginia in 1909, three years before the publication of *Landmarks in French Literature*, nine years before *Eminent Victorians* made him an eminent Edwardian.

The penniless Duncan Grant was a favored friend, recipient of her father's old trousers, years before recognition came to him as the foremost representative of Post-Impressionist painting in Britain.

The brilliant Maynard Keynes received invitations for weekends in Sussex long before he wrote *The Economic Consequences of the Peace*, an internationally influential book examining the failings of Georges Clemenceau, Woodrow Wilson and David Lloyd George at the Peace Conference in Paris.

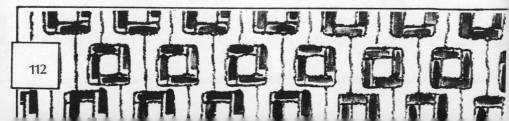

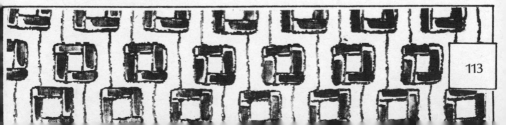

One exception was Roger Fry. Born in 1866, thirteen years older than Vanessa and sixteen years older than Virginia, Fry had achieved considerable eminence as an art critic before he became Vanessa's lover and Virginia's friend. In 1906 the American financier J. P. Morgan lured him to New York by arranging for his official appointment as Curator of Paintings at the Metropolitan Museum of Art. Unofficially he also served as Morgan's personal advisor on art purchases. Fry disliked this double assignment. He was also annoyed at Morgan's request to give slideshows for his mistress and his demand that Fry spend much of the year in New York. Preferring to take his chances, Fry quit his job and returned home.

In London he organized an exhibition in 1910 entitled "Manet and the Post-Impressionists." This show helped to bring Cezanne, Van Gogh, Gaugain, Matisse and Picasso to the attention of the British art public. The exhibition elicited expressions of outrage and contempt from outsiders toward those at the center of Bloomsbury.

For example, Wilfred Blunt, poet, diplomat, anti-imperialist, wrote these comments in his diary after visiting the Grafton Gallery:

"The exhibition is either an extremely bad joke or a swindle. Still less is there a trace of sense or skill or taste . . . Nothing but that gross puerility which scrawls indecencies on the walls of a privy . . ."

In later life appointed a Slade Professor at Cambridge, Fry was reputed to be the most important art critic since Ruskin. After he died, at his sister's request, Virginia agreed to write Fry's biography, then chafed at the task, not free to mention his love affair with Vanessa.

The homosexuality of so many Bloomsberries angered blood-and-guts macho men like D. H. Lawrence. Feeling sick after meeting Keynes, Duncan Grant and their friend, the charming Francis Birrell, Lawrence dreamt fitfully about black beetles and vowed to avoid future meetings with these men. After hearing Lawrence's nasty remarks, David Garnett, once friendly to both camps, cast his lot with Bloomsbury.

Dykes and Faggots, all of 'em!!

During World War I Bloomsbury pacifism became increasingly evident after introduction of the Military Service Bill. By 1916 most of Virginia's friends believed the official war goal favoring a fight to the finish no longer made any sense. They wanted to end the war as soon as possible, preferring a compromise peace arrived at by negotiation. It was a point of honor for Maynard and Lytton to oppose conscription. They would not fight in a war with unacceptable goals. The militarism Virginia lampoons in *Three Guineas* draws upon the experience of friends and her brother Adrian in fighting conscription.

Unhappy working at the Treasury for the Lloyd George government, Keynes told Duncan Grant, in 1917, "I work for a government I despise for ends I think criminal." Since the Treasury needed him the government quickly granted Keynes an exemption from military service. Leonard Woolf's exemption was medical. He suffered from an inherited nervous tremor, "quite uncontrollable," according to his sympathetic doctor.

The appeal fashioned by Lytton Strachey is now part of Anglo-American folklore. Initially Strachey sought to gain exemption by declaring himself a conscientious objector:

".... my feeling is directed not simply against the present war; I am convinced that the whole system by which it is sought to settle international disputes by force is profoundly evil . . . I should be doing wrong to take part in it."

This carefully reasoned initial request was denied.

For his next appearance before a Tribunal of eight, Strachey gave a theatrical performance demonstrating his unfitness for military service. Before the hearing a friend handed him an air cushion which he proceeded to inflate.

Placing it on a wooden bench, Strachey eased himself down on top of the cushion. This done, he carefully wrapped a tartan travelling rug around his knees. Now the invalid was ready to be interrogated by members of the Tribunal.

In an attempt to embarrass him one member asked if Strachey held a conscientious objection to all wars. "Oh no," came the piercing, high-pitched, distinctively Strachey voice, "not at all. Only this one."

"Then tell me, Mr. Strachey, what would you do if you saw a German soldier attempting to rape your sister?"

Strachey paused, making eye contact with two of his sisters who had accompanied him to the hearing. Then came his ribald answer with the double entendre, "I should try and get between them." The Tribunal did not appreciate his humor. Several days later, however, the military doctors examining Strachey declared him unfit for any kind of war service.

Duncan Grant and his friend David Garnett sought exemption by becoming farmers. At Wissett Lodge, a small village in Suffolk, they took over a vacant farmhouse with six acres attached to it. When the Central Tribunal notified them that their exemption would not be granted since they were self-employed, Vanessa travelled to the market town of Lewes, concluding arrangements there for Duncan and David to work as laborers at New House Farm. Virginia had sent Vanessa a description of a handsome farmhouse called Charleston which was only four miles from her home at Asheham. Vanessa rented Charleston, and immediately began turning it into a pleasant home, a task she and Duncan were to share for the rest of her life.

All the men within the inner circle of Bloomsbury managed to escape military conscription. Because of their rationalism they gained the enmity of traditionalists, those contentedly serving their country, accepting its sexual standards, worshipping the God of their fathers. Outside attacks further strengthened the bonds uniting Bloomsbury.

7.

THE
HOGARTH
PRESS

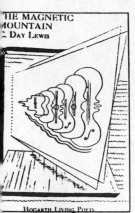

THE MAGNETIC
MOUNTAIN
C. DAY LEWIS

HOGARTH LIVING POETS

The Feather Bed
Robert Graves

TH ESSAYS
y Techniques
Poetry
E GRAVES

THE HOGARTH PRESS

Even Socialists like Virginia and Leonard Woolf harbor petit bourgeois dreams of turning a hobby into a flourishing capitalistic enterprise. Most people, unlike the Woolfs, never progress past the daydream to confront the myriad details that go along with owning and operating a business.

The Hogarth Press is a Horatio Alger success story. With much hard work, an educated nose for rooting out publishable manuscripts and almost no capital investment, the firm's list of titles grew stronger each year. In some respects, however, facts depart from legend: the heroes were not poor—Virginia being a modest heiress—or humble; the Woolfs, especially Leonard, were arrogant, convinced of their superior intellectual capacity. Occasionally they made mistakes, for example, turning down a chance to publish Ivy Compton-Burnet, but most of the time they guessed right when making judgments about authors without established reputations. The Hogarth Press is a monument the Woolfs created bearing testimony to their sound literary judgment.

123

Virginia had been interested in bookbinding as a young woman, but it was not until January 25, 1915, sitting at tea with Leonard, enjoying the celebration of her thirty-third birthday, that they planned three purchases: to buy a bulldog; to buy Hogarth House, a well-proportioned eighteenth century building in Richmond; and to buy a printing press.

It had been years since Virginia enjoyed such a happy birthday. Unfortunately her happiness did not last long. Within a month Virginia again began to hallucinate; talk became nonstop, wild, incoherent. By the time the Woolfs moved into Hogarth House, Leonard was employing four psychiatric nurses to care for her. Violent, screaming, out of control, Virginia directed much of her anger at him. In an effort to avoid giving offense, Leonard stayed away, scarcely seeing her during a two-month period.

Two years later, heavier, older-looking, having made progress in recovering from her illness, Virginia again began to think of buying a printing press. One major purpose of the press was therapeutic, to occupy Virginia with a simple constructive activity making no great mental demands. A second purpose was economic, to allow the Woolfs to publish their own work. The purchase of a small hand press would enable them to print limited editions of their short stories and offer them for sale to the general public.

Because of Virginia's illness their annual expenditures were high. Leonard's meager income did not come close to covering the cost of her medical expenses and their household expenses. To pay for the doctor bills Virginia sold some earrings and necklaces inherited from her mother. They were hardly a poor couple since they maintained two servants and two houses, one in Richmond and another in Sussex, but they were cautious in finding money to purchase the printing press.

On the day they unpacked the press at Hogarth House the Woolfs tingled with the excitement of children unwrapping birthday presents. They carried it up to the drawing room and soon discovered that one of the pieces was broken. Undaunted, they set about separating the blocks of types. Eager, unfamiliar with type, Virginia lost some letters in the carpet and mixed up some "h's" with the "n's." The challenge of mastering the new machine was so compelling that within a week Leonard was complaining to a friend about spending too much time at the press.

THREE   JEWS

By

LEONARD   WOOLF.

It was a Sunday and the first day of sprin
day on which one felt at any rate spring in the air. It
my window with its warm breath , with its inevitable
of sadness , I felt restless, and I had nowhere to go t
I knew was out of town. I looked out of my win
black trees breaking into bud, the tulips and the h
even London could not rub of their reds and blues
the delicate spring sunshine on the asphalt, and the
that the chimney pots broke into. I found mys
"damn it" for no very obvious reason. It was spri
the first stirring of the blood.

I wanted to see clean trees, and the
grass; I wanted flowers and leaves unsoiled by so
see and smell the earth; above all I wanted the ho

As partners and sole owners of The Hogarth Press, the Woolfs stated their intention of printing small books and pamphlets lacking commercial appeal for other publishers. Their first publication was a joint effort, two short stories, appropriately titled *Two Stories*, "The Mark on the Wall" by Virginia and "Three Jews" by Leonard. They planned to sell the book by sending out circulars announcing its availability to friends and acquaintances. After pressing an edition of 150 copies, they selected gay Japanese paper for the covers and offered Publication No. 1 for sale. Leonard and Virginia were members of the Fabian Society, and two of their Fabian friends, Beatrice Webb and Charlotte Shaw were among the early purchasers of *Two Stories*.

18   THREE JEWS

"Dad, I want to marry a girl'—a really nice girl—"but she's not one of us: will you give me your permission and blessing?" Well I don't believe in it. Our women are as good, better than Christian women. Aren't they as beautiful, as clever, as good wives? I know my poor mother, God rest her soul, used to say: "My son," she said, "if you come to me and say you want to marry a good girl, a Jewess, I don't care whether she hasn't a chemise to her back, I'll welcome her—but if you marry a Christian, if she's as rich as Solomon, I've done with you—don't you ever dare to come into my house again." Vell, I don't go as far as that, though I understand it. Times change: I might have received his wife, even though she was a Goy. But a servant girl who washed my dishes! I couldn't do it. One must have some dignity."

He stood there upright, stern, noble: a battered scarred old rock, but immovable under his seedy black coat. I couldn't offer him a shilling; I shook his hand, and left him brooding over his son and his graves.

THE MARK ON THE WALL
By
VIRGINIA WOOLF

Perhaps it was the middle of January in the present year that I first looked up and saw the mark on the wall. In order to fix a date it is necessary to remember what one saw. So now I think of the fire; the steady film of yellow light upon the page of my book; the three chrysanthemums in the round glass bowl on the mantelpiece. Yes, it must have been the winter time, and we had just finished our tea, for I remember that I was smoking a cigarette when I looked up and saw the mark on the wall for the first time. I looked up through the smoke of my cigarette and my eye lodged for a moment upon the burning coals, and that old fancy of the crimson flag flapping from the castle tower came into my mind, and I thought of the cavalcade of red knights riding up the side of the black rock. Rather to my relief the sight of the mark interrupted the fancy, for it is an old fancy, an automatic

Katherine Mansfield was the first author unrelated to the Woolfs whom they published. Virginia admired her work, and Mansfield agreed to have *Prelude*, one of her stories, become Publication No. 2.

Another early publication was a small, private memorial edition of *Poems* by Leonard's brother Cecil, killed in action in World War I. Another brother Philip was wounded in the same battle.

The first big book order for the press was in 1919 following the publication of *Kew Gardens*, a short story by Virginia. An anonymous reviewer had strongly recommended it in the *Times Literary Supplement*. Upon returning from a weekend at their country home, the Woolfs were surprised to find the hall table covered with 150 mail orders from unknown customers and bookstores throughout the country.

Virginia's feeling of success was somewhat dampened by the need to prepare 90 copies for immediate distribution, to cut up covers and glue down the backs, and then to help bundle and address the packages. *Kew Gardens* sold so well that the Woolfs were forced to order an outside printing of 500 copies. Another book printed in 1919 which sold well was *Poems* by their friend Tom Eliot.

Despite its remarkable success The Hogarth Press always retained the character of a Mom-and-Pop publishing house. The office remained in the basement of their homes, first at Hogarth House and then at Tavistock Square in Bloomsbury. Leonard tested the limits of economy for employees by cutting up and using old galley proofs as a substitute for toilet paper. There were few frills, no specialized staff positions. Every employee was expected to pitch in and do everything necessary to meet emergencies. Leonard kept the staff lean and trim. This was no fat bureaucracy, idling away time, overstaffed and underused.

Woolf proved himself something of a tyrant, especially with male employees, once greeting a young man, watch in hand, bitterly complaining about his arrival at the office two minutes late.

Meticulous, penurious, unable to control his rage over accounts that were off a penny or two, Leonard had trouble retaining young, well-educated male employees for long periods of time. Being a boss brought out the worst in him. His penny-pinching also lost some successful authors who would have further increased the profits of the firm. What he did best of all, and what he prided himself on, was the ability to fill book orders promptly and to gauge the amount of stock needed on the shelves.

Virginia admired his efficiency, comparing him to the mowing machines farmers used: "round and round they go, without haste without rest, until finally the little square of corn in the middle is cut and all is done." Virginia helped out with the production from time to time but left most of the business decisions in his hands. Her main contribution was editorial.

The firm of Duckworth and Company, owned by her stepbrother Gerald, published Virginia's first two novels, *The Voyage Out* and *Night and Day*. In time The Hogarth Press acquired re-publication rights to both these books and eventually published all of her novels, her collected essays, and other works such as *Flush* and *Orlando*.

Efficient Mowing Machine

After the Press was established Virginia
Woolf never again had to worry about
writing to please a publisher. She was free
to experiment, to push up against the
rigidity of traditional forms, to select new
approaches to the craft of fiction solely
on the basis of their appeal to her artistic
judgment. Although freed from the necessity
of conforming to publishers' tastes,
Virginia continued to worry about
the critics' reception to her works. For years
this kind of worry plagued her, causing
anguish and anxiety long after she
acquired a reputation as a successful
novelist, critic and essayist.

With a combined income derived from sales of Virginia's books and profits from the Press, the Woolfs were able to buy things that made their life more comfortable. Virginia ordered four comfortable chairs without worrying about the cost. Monks House was enlarged, a room added for her use. Leonard employed a gardener and indulged his taste for exotic plants. With Leonard as chauffeur Virginia loved touring on the Continent in a secondhand car they bought. She gave her niece Angelica a quarterly allowance. One of her friends was to introduce her to Elizabeth Arden's beauty parlor. Playfully she anticipated the outcome of the visit: "Fingers to be red. Toes to be silver. Face to be lifted; nose to be filled with wax." Even with these indulgences the Woolfs spent much less than they earned, keeping many of their old frugal ways instead of living a life of luxury.

Another benefit from the Press was the opportunity it gave the Woolfs to expand their acquaintanceship beyond the world of literature. In the 1920's the Press took over publication of the International Psycho-analytical Library and published an authorized English translation of Freud's papers, and later, the standard edition of his collected work. To escape the Nazi menace, the Freud family fled to England after the Anschluss, and in 1939 the Woolfs visited Dr. Freud at his home in Maresfield Gardens, Hampstead. Eighty-two years old, suffering from cancer of the jaw, Freud was still the courtly Viennese, presenting Virginia with a narcissus, not in any way intended to signify his assessment of her personality. She found him alert, a "screwed up shrunk very old man," the fire within flickering now, but nearing extinction.

One of the disadvantages of the Press was having fights with relatives about publication. On occasion the Woolfs demonstrated a need to suspend their critical judgment in order to keep peace within the family. For example, the Woolfs printed some work by their nephew Julian, although both seriously doubted its merit. As a publisher Virginia concluded, "He is no poet," but as Julian's aunt, and as Vanessa's sister, she urged Leonard to reconsider his objections. Virginia was caught between her husband on one side and her sister and nephew on the other. On another occasion she recalled turning her sister into a tiger, growling in a cave, by refusing to publish Julian's essay on Roger Fry.

In retaliation Julian, then teaching in China, stopped writing to his aunt for six months.

Most of the time they took the hard road, refusing to publish friends' work that did not meet their standards.

From 1919 to 1939 the Hogarth Press published an impressive list of authors, introducing several to English readers. Here is a partial listing of authors published by the Press:

W. H. Auden, Ivan Bunin, T. S. Eliot, E. M. Forster, Sigmund Freud, Roger Fry, Robert Graves, Christopher Isherwood, Maynard Keynes, Harold Laski, John Lehmann, Rosamond Lehmann, C. D. Lewis, Katherine Mansfield, Edwin Muir, J. Middleton Murry, Benito Mussolini, William Plomer, Herbert Read, Rainer Maria Rilke, A. L. Rowse, Vita Sackville-West, Edith Sitwell, Logan Pearsall Smith, Stephen Spender, Laurens van der Post, H. G. Wells, Rebecca West, Leonard Woolf, Virginia Woolf.

Complete Catalogue of the Hogarth Press

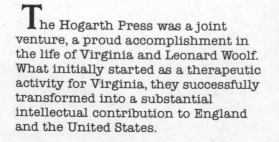

The Hogarth Press was a joint venture, a proud accomplishment in the life of Virginia and Leonard Woolf. What initially started as a therapeutic activity for Virginia, they successfully transformed into a substantial intellectual contribution to England and the United States.

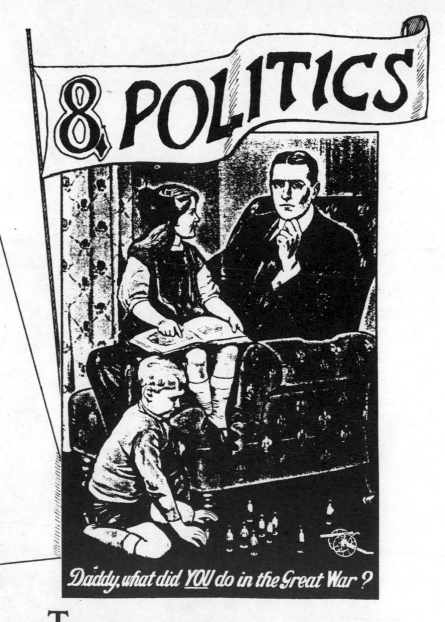

8 POLITICS

Daddy, what did _YOU_ do in the Great War?

The breadth of Virginia Woolf's interests becomes evident when her political and literary achievements are set side by side. In her diaries and collected letters readers can observe her strong interest in political issues and her many references to political affairs. She refused to simplify ideas, to overlook troublesome aspects of political problems in order to avoid reexamining decisions that previously had seemed resolved.

Many critics write about Virginia Woolf, the novelist and essayist, oftentimes neglecting Virginia Woolf, the political scientist and anthropologist. Although generally known for his careful guarding of her reputation, Leonard himself helped create a misunderstanding about the significance of politics in her life.

As a novelist she paid special attention to the personal life of politicians whenever she had a chance to meet them and pump them for information, eager to gather material for use in her fiction. For this reason Leonard characterized her in his autobiography as "the least political animal that has ever lived since Aristotle invented the definition."

'. . . the least political animal that has ever lived since Aristotle invented the definition."

Having set this false hare loose, he immediately started to chase after it, warning readers in the next sentence that his wife "was not a bit like the Virginia Woolf who appears . . . as a frail invalidish lady living in an ivory tower in Bloomsbury and worshipped by a little clique of aesthetes."

No Rapunsel, her!
No Ivory Tower, here!

The richness of her political life needs no defense from Leonard, or from anyone else willing to look at the record.

One of her early political acts was a highly successful attempt in 1910 that embarrassed the British Home Fleet by making it the butt of an elaborate hoax. Virginia, along with her brother Adrian who enacted the role of translator, and four other friends were piped on board H.M.S. *Dreadnought* while pretending to be members of a diplomatic mission from Ethiopia. Appearing in blackface, sporting a full beard, her ankles covered by a caftan that swept to the deck and hair hidden beneath a saucy turban adding an inch or two to her height, the androgynous Virginia was cast in the role of native prince. Completely taken in by the disguise, the crew, along with the Flag Commander, who happened to be her cousin Herbert Fisher, gave the bogus party a royal welcome, including a full tour of the ship.

She enjoyed poking fun at the Navy, showing up the inflexibility of this completely masculine enterprise, exposing the narrowness of the military mind, so closed off from reality it failed to recognize garbled lines of Latin taken from the *Aeneid* which Adrian had dredged up from boyhood memory in a frantic effort to sound like an Ethiopian. Luckily, the one sailor familiar with Swahili was not on board ship at the time of the visit.

The little party's puncture of masculinity and militarism was similar in some respects to the prankishness of Lytton Strachey, who later was to deflate the reputation of Dr. Thomas Arnold, Headmaster of Rugby, General Charles Gordon, Cardinal Manning and Florence Nightingale in his highly successful biography of *Eminent Victorians*. Many Edwardians were eager to hold up to ridicule Victorian heroes and their patriarchical institutions.

Years later Virginia still enjoyed recalling the adventure for the amusement of her friends. Eventually she prevailed upon Adrian, who rarely wrote anything, to prepare his account of *the Dreadnought Hoax*, which The Hogarth Press published in the thirties.

Virginia's interest in political affairs and her commitment to helping those less fortunate than she was much more serious than this once-in-a-lifetime leg pull of the British Navy. As a shy young woman growing to maturity in the first decade of the century, she did not feel capable of either arguing or speaking up in public. Wanting to aid the cause of women's suffrage, she volunteered to do the humbler kind of work needed to support the campaign and was assigned the task of addressing envelopes.

EQUALITY

M·B·WALKER

She stuck to the job without much pleasure. While working in the Adult suffrage office, she observed that it was filled with ardent, educated young women. Suddenly she felt as if she had stepped inside an H. G. Wells novel. What distressed her was a growing awareness of the "inhuman side" of politics, the side that shrivelled all the best feelings and attracted "bloodless women who don't care for their own relations."

From time to time Virginia expressed feelings of loathing toward certain women which appear as acid-burned etchings in her diaries and letters. Despite these highly personal, biting remarks about particular women, Virginia spent time working to extend the political and social rights of women.

Upon the urging of a friend, Virginia, then in her twenties, agreed to teach a course at Morley College, a night school for workers in South London. She was serious about her teaching, insisting on the need for a course in English history, knowing full well it would be unpopular with students. Of the eight students registered for the course, half quickly dropped out leaving four working women who attended regularly.

At each session she came prepared to teach, anxious to give her students an introduction that would serve as a solid foundation for their future studies. The young, headstrong teacher did not back away from raising questions about the value for her students of a course the headmistress was prepared to offer on the French Revolution. She felt they were not ready to absorb a series of eight lectures that would drop into their mind "like meteors from another sphere impinging on this planet." Virginia considered the lectures would be too much like "disconnected fragments" to be useful to the students.

THE FABIANS

Leonard introduced her to the Fabian
Society, a group of socialists known for their
devotion to gradualism and the superior
intellectual leadership provided by such
members of the Old Gang as Bernard Shaw,
the Webbs (Beatrice and Sidney), and
Sydney Olivier. Virginia was not particularly
active in the Fabian Society. She spent much
more time serving as secretary of the
Rodmell Labour Party when the Woolfs
lived at Monks House; when they lived
in Richmond, a branch of the
Women's Co-operative Guild met
regularly at Hogarth House.

Her minor role as a grassroots worker for socialism and socialist
causes contrasted sharply with Leonard's high-level contribution to
the development of policy for the Labour Party and his service on
executive committees. Before the start of World War I the Webbs
had spotted him as a bright young man who might be useful to
the Fabian Research Bureau. Much of one of his early reports on
International Government, commissioned by the Webbs, was
incorporated virtually intact into the British Draft Covenant on
the League of Nations.

Besides her engagement in political affairs Virginia also wrote articles and delivered talks for such labor organizations as the *Daily Worker*, the Artists' International Association, the Workers' Educational Association, and the Women's Co-operative Guild. In three of these essays published as "The Leaning Tower," "The Artist and Politics," and "Memories of a Working Women's Guild," Virginia Woolf becomes a political scientist, pointing out the significance of social structure, particularly social class, for the subjugation of women and the creativity of artists and writers.

Design of William Morris

"Why," she asks in "The Leaning Tower," "should a family, like the Shelleys, like the Keatses, like the Brontës, suddenly burst into flame and bring to birth Shelley, Keats and the Brontës?" Like a professor of sociology she asks, "What are the conditions that bring about that explosion?"

148

Before presenting the theory she prefers, Virginia notes serious gaps in the scientific knowledge currently available: The germ of influenza is yet to be discovered. How then can one expect to discover the germ of genius? Other explanations of genius proposed by scientists are not fully satisfactory to her.

" To the psychologists a writer is an oyster; feed him on gritty facts, irritate him with ugliness . . . and he will produce a pearl. The genealogists say that certain stocks . . . breed writers as fig trees breed figs—Dryden, Swift, and Pope . . . were all cousins. "

Mystique

Her theory accounting for the development of genius is firmly based on differences in social class. Almost all of the writers who have made superlative contributions to literature have been the beneficiaries of "middle-class birth and expensive education;" their "parents' station" in life and their "parents' gold" gave those with talent the time and training needed to develop their craft.

PARENTAL GOLD

GENIUS AT PLAY

Her sociological explanation makes no case for the continued support of the current state of affairs. What she is intent on doing is pointing out the significance of social class upon the development of England's best writers, those we reread for no other reason than that they speak to us in voices that we trust.

Her essays on the sociology of art are less remembered today than *A Room of One's Own* and *Three Guineas*, two books that helped raise the consciousness of women in the twenties and thirties. In these works she identifies various social institutions that support patriarchic control and exposes the efforts of men to keep women subjugated. Here she becomes an anthropologist, analyzing the relationship between social structure and dress, ridiculing medals and ribbons of honor, university hoods and academic gowns, comparing the rites of savages with those of military officers and college professors.

Over and over again she uncovers different forms of exploitation that men inflict upon women—within the home in their roles as brother, father, husband—outside of it in their roles as teacher, politician, employer. She persisted in writing these books, knowing full well that her challenging thesis would provoke opposition from those in her circle of Bloomsbury friends.

Virginia Woolf understood the significance of politics in shaping the careers of women and artists; in deed and word she struggled to help them gain their rightful place in society.

THE LAST YEARS

Virginia Woolf's suicide poses this riddle: Why would a successful novelist and critic surrounded by a circle of loving friends and relatives commit suicide? Why would a wife with a devoted husband anxious to protect her and care for her needs take her own life?

Work and love, according to Freud, are the two most important activities in life. Virginia seemed blessed in both areas. She was a highly disciplined, productive author. Every morning she spent three hours writing. After lunch she usually worked at the less demanding aspects of her craft, perhaps reading proof for books and articles accepted for publication, or revising and typing handwritten pages composed during the morning.

Her work brought fame and respect. On the basis of her publications, the Prime Minister was prepared in 1935 to recommend to His Majesty her appointment to the Companion of Honour, the kind of recognition granted to few women of that time. She refused the offer, considering such awards "damned nonsense" holding them up to ridicule in *Three Guineas*.

By the 1930's Virginia Woolf's novels had won international acclaim. In 1937 *The Years* soon climbed to the top of the bestseller list in the United States. Her novels received front-page reviews on both sides of the Atlantic. American editors, anxious to increase their circulation, made attractive offers to purchase her short stories and critical essays. Her "thimble of vanity" overflowed at Maynard Keynes' praise for a centenary article marking the birth of the English historian Edward Gibbon. Keynes said it was twenty times better than any other critical work devoted to Gibbon.

Virginia's domestic life was unclouded by scandal or gossip about Leonard's conduct as a husband. He was attentive and ever vigilant, protecting her from the intrusion of friends, warding off excessive social obligations, even lying on occasion to help her maintain her spirit and productivity. She continued seeing members of Old Bloomsbury and enjoyed renewing intimate ties at meetings of The Memoir Club. In addition, nieces and nephews, now old enough to leave home and strike out on their own, enlivened family visits at Charleston and Monks House by telling her tales of love and the trials of new careers. Her life was rich, deep, at times full to overflowing.

Upon closer examination her later life, when judged from her own perspective, contained hidden pockets of darkness, reasons for sadness, even despair. Having volunteered as an ambulance driver, her nephew Julian Bell was killed in the Spanish Civil War. His death was a devastating loss, most of all to his mother. Shattered, Vanessa took to her bed for days. Virginia stayed with her in London, helping ease her pain, ministering to her needs, bringing her round again to the routine rhythm of life.

Old friends had died: Lytton Strachey and Roger Fry; Janet Case, who had tutored her in Greek at her home in Hyde Park Gate; Lady Ottoline Morrell, whose salon she had attended at Garsington Manor and Gower Street. Virginia wrote the women's obituaries for the *Times*.

In 1939, soon after the start of World War II, suicide was a subject close to her consciousness. As a Jew Leonard was more deeply affected by the Nazi threat of invasion than was Virginia. Waiting for the war to begin he compared his life to "one of those terrible nightmares in which one tries to flee from some malignant, nameless . . . horror." After the battle for Britain began the war was brought close to home as they watched air battles fought over the Ouse Valley. In London the Luftwaffe's attacks partially destroyed their home and the office of the Hogarth Press at Tavistock Square and Mecklenburgh Square.

The Woolfs managed to salvage
thousands of books, some from her
father's library, some accumulated since
her marriage to Leonard, still others
printed by The Hogarth Press. They transferred
many of them to Monks House where,
helter-skelter, they stood in shaky piles on
tables, and chairs, multi-volume sets of
English and French classics bound in calf,
now grimy, jumbled about like a group of
displaced refugees. The chaos in the
house did little to calm either Virginia
or Leonard.

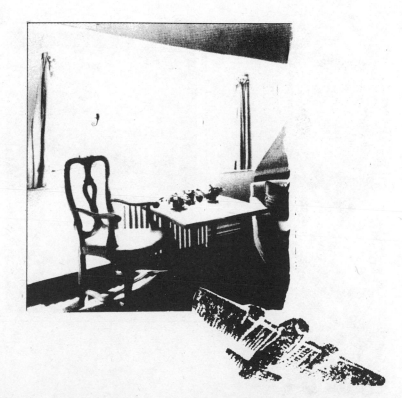

Her brother Adrian decided he would commit suicide rather than submit himself to Hitler's brutality. As a physician he had ready access to lethal doses of poison, which he offered to make available to Leonard and Virginia. After the German invasion of the Lowlands, the Woolfs also talked of committing suicide by closing their garage doors and starting up their automobile engine. Upon further reflection Virginia decided she did not want to die, confiding to her diary, "I don't want the garage to see the end of me. I've a wish for 10 years more and to write my book . . ."

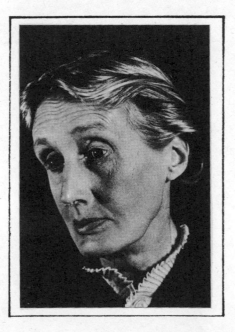

Apparently, even more troubling than the war was her uncertainty about gauging the true value of her literary work. Like many people private affairs had a greater emotional impact on her life than public catastrophes. "One old lady pinning on her cap" she wrote "has more reality" than all the bombast resulting from the war.

Doubts about her novels had a long history preceding the start of World War II.

In 1936 revising *The Years* she saw the needle of assessment swing wildly back and forth; one day her novel was "feeble twaddle . . . such twilight gossip . . . such a show up of my own decrepitude . . ." Dipping into it again the next morning, she changed her opinion. Overnight it had become "a full, bustling live book . . . I think there's something to it." Once again, two months later it was "a complete failure . . ." followed by yet another reassessment: "Yesterday I read it again and I think it may be my best book." These rapid, wide swings in critical judgment caused her acute despair, further battering a confidence perched on shaky pilings.

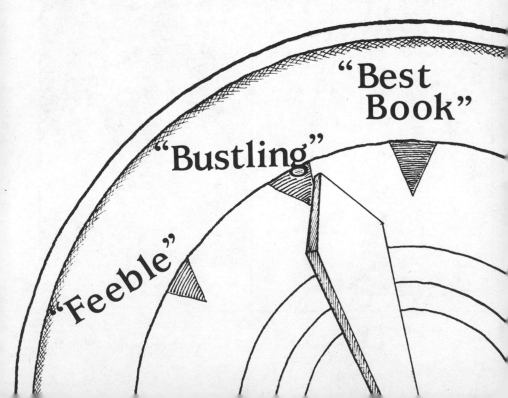

Courage was the virtue Virginia most admired. She herself displayed great courage, continuing to write without the confidence an author needs to string words together. To keep writing while her "head . . . was still all nerve," she devised an invalid's schedule; rest after lunch, and "reading only with the skin of the eye." One false move meant "racing despair, exaltation and all the rest of that familiar misery."

"Live"

"Twaddle"

On February 26, 1941 she finished writing *Between the Acts* and handed the typescript to Leonard. He was delighted with it and recommended publication. Virginia had not suffered through this last novel; on the contrary she had enjoyed writing almost every page. After rereading it her satisfaction disappeared. Her latest opinion was that *Between the Acts* needed extensive revision. This shifting evaluation recalled the wide oscillations in her critical assessment of *The Years*. She now felt it would be a mistake to publish her "so called novel," deeming it "much too slight and sketchy."

In March 1941, the month in which she committed suicide, Virginia made only two entries in her diary; neither makes any mention of or allusion to the possibility of suicide. When she first conceived the plan is unknown. Her silence is understandable. Those seriously intending to commit suicide seldom discuss their plan with others, since most confidants entrusted with the news try either to dissuade them, or to take measures preventing them from carrying out their plan.

THE HIGH PRIESTESS

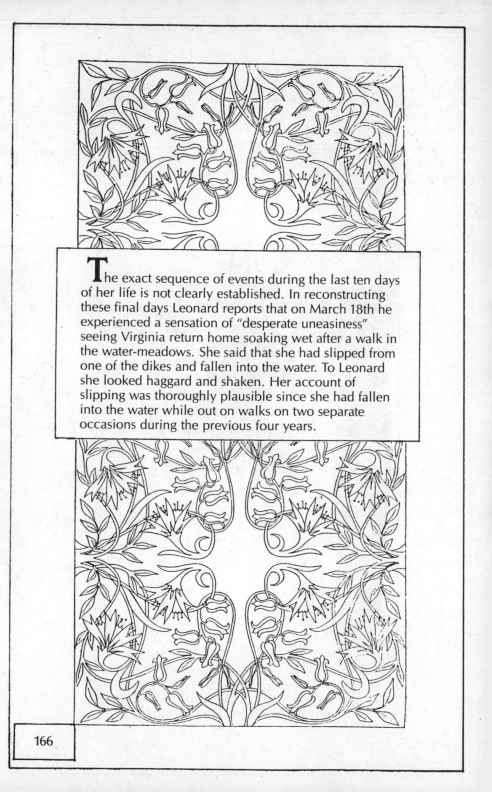

The exact sequence of events during the last ten days of her life is not clearly established. In reconstructing these final days Leonard reports that on March 18th he experienced a sensation of "desperate uneasiness" seeing Virginia return home soaking wet after a walk in the water-meadows. She said that she had slipped from one of the dikes and fallen into the water. To Leonard she looked haggard and shaken. Her account of slipping was thoroughly plausible since she had fallen into the water while out on walks on two separate occasions during the previous four years.

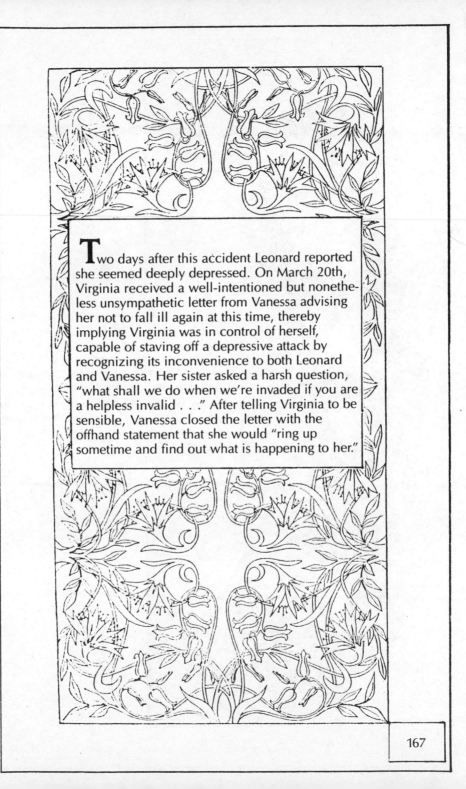

Two days after this accident Leonard reported she seemed deeply depressed. On March 20th, Virginia received a well-intentioned but nonetheless unsympathetic letter from Vanessa advising her not to fall ill again at this time, thereby implying Virginia was in control of herself, capable of staving off a depressive attack by recognizing its inconvenience to both Leonard and Vanessa. Her sister asked a harsh question, "what shall we do when we're invaded if you are a helpless invalid . . ." After telling Virginia to be sensible, Vanessa closed the letter with the offhand statement that she would "ring up sometime and find out what is happening to her."

In separate suicide notes to Leonard and Vanessa, Virginia told of hearing voices again, of not being able to concentrate on her work. She was convinced she was making Leonard unhappy, that he could do his work better without taking the trouble to care for her. Her final conclusion was, "I can't go on spoiling your life any longer."

On Friday morning, March 28, Leonard was at Monks House working in the garden when Virginia left for a walk. When he entered the house to join her for lunch, he found a suicide letter on the mantelpiece in the living room. After reading it he ran down to the River Ouse, desperately searching for her in the meadows. He was too late.

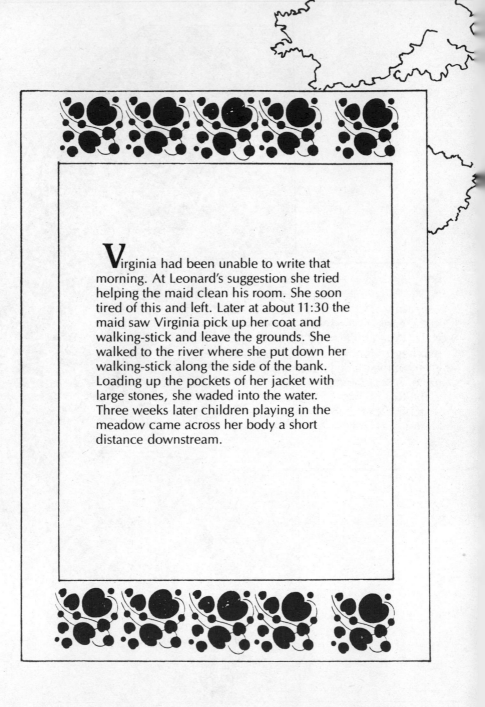

Virginia had been unable to write that morning. At Leonard's suggestion she tried helping the maid clean his room. She soon tired of this and left. Later at about 11:30 the maid saw Virginia pick up her coat and walking-stick and leave the grounds. She walked to the river where she put down her walking-stick along the side of the bank. Loading up the pockets of her jacket with large stones, she waded into the water. Three weeks later children playing in the meadow came across her body a short distance downstream.

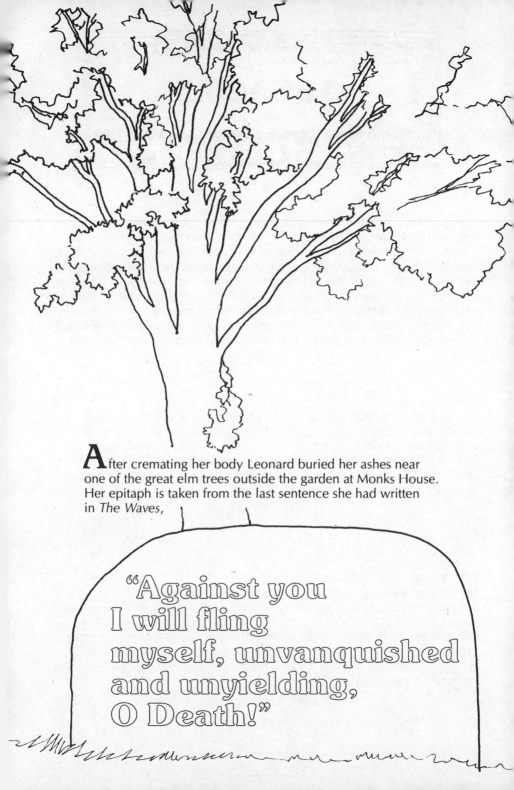

After cremating her body Leonard buried her ashes near one of the great elm trees outside the garden at Monks House. Her epitaph is taken from the last sentence she had written in *The Waves,*

"Against you
I will fling
myself, unvanquished
and unyielding,
O Death!"

LEGACIES

"Virginia Woolf was the centre not merely of an esoteric group, but of the literary life of London. Her position was due to a concurrence of qualities and circumstances which never happened before, and which I do not think will ever happen again. It maintained the dignified and admirable tradition of Victorian upper middle-class culture—a situation in which the artist was neither the servant of the exalted patron, the parasite of the plutocrat, nor the entertainer of the mob—a situation in which the producer and the consumer of art were on an equal footing, ... With the death of Virginia Woolf, a whole pattern of culture is broken ..."

T. S. ELIOT

". . . she was irradiated in my eyes with the halo of having written *Jacob's Room*, *To the Lighthouse* and *Mrs. Dalloway*. No other books seemed to me to express with anything like the same penetration and beauty the sensibility of our age . . . almost everything else seemed, after I read them, utterly wide of the target and inadequately aware of what was needed."

JOHN LEHMANN

"There is an important reversal of values revealed in Virginia Woolf's novels, for the shape that emerges is a fundamentally poetic one. They are not primarily held together by a framework of socio-historical, moral or psychological concepts, nor by the literary forms with which these were traditionally associated . . . Everything is subordinated to poetry and to its mysterious healing power, to its power to draw together, if only temporarily, the echoes and fragments with which our experience reverberates."

JOHN MEPHAM

"... human life was her theme ... She did not want to scratch about on the surface, to glue incidents together into plots ... She wanted to reveal the springs of action."

BERNARD BLACKSTONE

"... she gave us a new interest in life, a new way of looking at life ... Even at this distance in time, I can say without any exaggeration she was the most remarkable human being I have ever known."

NIGEL NICOLSON

"... I always thought her genius led her by short cuts to some essential point which everybody else had missed. She did not walk there: she sprang ... She and Coleridge both seem to me to combine the unusually mixed ingredients of genius and intellect, the wild, fantastic, intuitive genius on the one hand, and the cold reasoning intellect on the other."

VITA SACKVILLE-WEST

"She instantly convinced my generation of her genius and I was also impressed by her originality. Because, of course, the attempts made to show that she derived from other writers ... ignore chronology. The tendency to 'the stream of consciousness' technique was general, but she was as early as anyone in applying it."

REBECCA WEST

"*Kew Gardens*, and *The Mark on the Wall* (are) ... lovely little things; her style trails after her as she walks and talks, catching up dust and grass in its folds ... we have something more elusive than had yet been achieved in English."

E. M. FORSTER

"*To the Lighthouse* is in three movements. It has been called a novel in sonata form, and certainly the slow central section, conveying the passing of time, does demand a musical analogy. We have, when reading it, the rare pleasure of inhabiting two worlds at once, a pleasure only art can give: the world where a little boy wants to go to a lighthouse but never manages it until, with changed emotions, he goes there as a young man ..."

E. M. FORSTER

"Virginia Woolf was aware of course of routines. But they seemed to her strange . . . They were also particularly associated in her mind with the male sex. The man, rather than the woman, was a creature of routine. The more he excelled at it the more absurd he appeared in Virginia Woolf's eye; so that a highly successful man who became Prime Minister, or an admiral, was like a creature with bright golden chains not only hung on him but visibly running all through him."

STEPHEN SPENDER

"*The Waves* is a prose poem about the group of friends whose lives, from birth almost, play to one another like the instruments in quartet or quintet . . . It seems to me a book of great beauty and a prose poem of genius. *The Waves* is essentially a religious or mystical work, a poem about vision, prayer, poetry itself . . ."

STEPHEN SPENDER

"*Orlando* is, among other things, a hybrid produced by the modern mind—parodic, rhapsodic, biographic, fantastic, prosaic, poetic."

MARIA DIBATTISTA

"Never was a book more feminine, more recklessly feminine. It may be labelled clever and shrewd, mocking, suggestive, subtle, 'modern', but these terms do not convey the spirit of it—which essentially is feminine. That quality is of course indescribable."

TIMES LITERARY SUPPLEMENT REVIEW
OF *The Voyage Out*